Overshadowed

The Power of Our Testimony

A DISCIPLESHIP TOOL

by

Dianne M. Hartshorn

Dear Sara,
God is overshadowing you!
Love to you,
Dianne

Name: Dianne M. Hall
Title: Overshadowed: The Power of Our Testimony,
A Discipleship Tool
By Dianne M. Hall

ISBN: 978-1-952369-41-4
Subjects: 1. Religion/General
2. Religion/Christianity/Personal Growth
3. Religion/Christianity/General

Cover design: Krystine Kercher
Editing: Linda Gilden

Published by EA Books Publishing, a division of Living Parables of Central Florida, Inc. a 501c3 EABooksPublishing.com

DEDICATION

To Jesus Christ, my Lord and Savior.

To our beloved angel boy Drew, who is healed,

running, and dancing with Jesus in the glories of heaven.

January 16, 2001 — February 26, 2020

WE ARE BECAUSE YOU WERE

But as it is written: "Eye has not seen, nor ear heard, Nor have entered into the heart of man the things which God has prepared for those who love Him." But God has revealed them to us through His Spirit. For the Spirit searches all things, yes, the deep things of God.
1 Corinthians 2:9-10 (NKJV)

Contents

Acknowledgements

Thank you, Lord Jesus, for rescuing me and my family. Draw me and we will run after You. Thank you, Holy Spirit, for guidance and direction in all things.

To all the Saints who wrote their personal testimonies. Tony, Rose, Steve and Beth, Christie, Chris and Jessie and Evelyn. You are giving from your hearts to build faith in the Body of Christ. I bless you for sharing your stories. Thank you.

To my Marine husband, who was stretched to the max with this project. Perseverance prevailed. I am so glad we function as a team. I love that you are leaving a legacy to our children that will not fade away. Thanks, Pastor Babe. I love you!

Thank you to my new friend Martha Kelfer Allen. May God bless the work of your hands.

To Cheri Cowell and your staff at EABooks Publishing. I met Cheri at several Speak Up Conferences. Cheri encouraged me many times when I felt like giving up this publishing process.

Linda Gilden, your developmental editing became a great asset in my life. Thank you, Dara Lehner. I appreciate your great talents. The setbacks didn't deter us! Praise the Lord.

Thanks to my phenomenal family who give me inspiration and encouragement in ways they don't even realize. We lost one of our precious grandchildren as I was writing this book. We miss you Drew but love the thought of you running free now. We gained a granddaughter from a marriage made in heaven. Anthony and Hannah, your wedding was a gift for all of us. We welcomed a precious sixteen year old into our family, too. I know the blessing of seeing my children's children. Thank you, Lord, for the blessing and the expansion of our forever family. Anthony, Hannah, Katelyn, Natalia,

i

Kyalie, Drew, Emily, Logan, Reagan, Bryce, Ruthie, Bennet, and MJ. Thank you for loving me, dear grandchildren!

Thanks to Pastor Cal Garcia and Sandy. The Word of God goes forth with power from Auburn Hills Christian Center and we are so thankful for all you do in the Kingdom of God. Blessings!

To Pastor Duane Vander Klok and Jeanie, all the pastors and staff. Thank you for casting vision. God bless you for the Word that reaches the world from ResLife Church in Grandville, MI.

Thanks to the She Speaks Conference in Charlotte, North Carolina, for the professional training I received. This is where my book-writing commenced and creativity blossomed. Blessings!

Thanks to Carol Kent and the Speak Up Conference in Grand Rapids, MI. for the excellent training I received — the fellowship was delightful!

Thanks to the Breathe Christian Writers Conference in Grand Rapids, MI. You exude inspiration!

Biblical Worldview Topics

Introduction

Allow me to take you on a journey where you will see how darkness turns into light; sickness becomes health; poverty merges into provision; heartbreak yields to comfort; unbelief disintegrates, and faith flows freely; weakness becomes strength; chaos is demolished, and stability arises; depression is defeated, and joy bubbles up.

This is more than a new year or a new season. This is a new era where we will see the "restoration of all things." We look at the turmoil that the entire population of planet earth is experiencing and shake our heads in wonder. Our world doesn't look like it is being restored. Our eyes behold: a Chinese virus spreading into a worldwide pandemic, economic disaster, closed schools, unemployment numbers similar to a depression, businesses gone, restaurants closed, and the rioting and burning of American cities. What can this mean?

The whole world needs restoration, and the Bible has answers for us. "Faith is the substance of things hoped for, the evidence of things not seen," God speaks of the restoration of all things, think of that! Have you been waiting for God to restore your life? You can choose to enter this new era with a brand new vision! Will you allow the Most High God to:

- Restart and reset your life? Your business?
- Restore a relationship, a marriage, a family, a prodigal?
- Renew your mind and revive your soul?
- Lead you to repentance and to receive forgiveness?

I decree and proclaim this new era is the beginning of restoring all things for your life. God is omniscient and has every answer you need. The only way to live through these challenging days is to be overshadowed by God's mighty power.

The book *Overshadowed* delves into the promises we have from God mapped out in the Word of God.

Jesus came to give us truth. The truth that will set us free. Jesus wanted His disciples to pray and not give up. We live by faith in the Son of God who loved us and died for us.

My goal in writing this book is to encourage you in your faith. We need our faith stirred constantly. When Jesus returns, He will be looking for faith on the earth. Where? Faith living in our hearts. That applies whether you are a new believer just starting your faith walk or if you have walked with Jesus for many years. What is the result of our faith being stirred? The chaos and deception will not shake you in the world.

Overshadowed has three main emphases: to amplify, to increase, and to magnify.

First, I want to amplify the stories of people in the Bible who were changed. Let's look closer together! God overshadows Zechariah and his wife Elizabeth; Mary, the mother of Jesus, and Joseph, Mary's husband. Their testimonies show how God's glory came to the earth when God sent His Son in the fullness of time.

Second, I want to increase the emphasis on ordinary Christians living in today's world who have experienced change. God overshadowed their lives, too, just like the characters in the Bible. God sets regular people apart for His Kingdom. Their testimonies developed amid chaos. There is power in their testimonies because they conquered. God can do that for you.

Third, I want to magnify God's Word because of its power to change our lives. Get ready to search the Scriptures with me!

I asked several believers to write their testimonies so that I could compile them into this book. I have laughed, cried, worshipped, and rejoiced with the people on these pages. Their stories are true. Some of the names are pseudonyms. Each one has been rescued by God's hand in a different way and at various stages of their lives. These are not fables, fantasy, or fiction. They are ordinary people with daily routines: working jobs, raising families, and experiencing commonplace events. They may be called "ordinary" by the world, but the Bible refers to them as "saints." I used to think that saints were dead holy people, but the Bible speaks of living saints, disciples of Jesus Christ.

Let me introduce you to:

> *Tony* — I asked my husband to write his testimony. Sometimes our children do not know the story of how we came to Christ. Part of our legacy to our children is telling them our personal story of salvation. I met Tony at Michigan State University after he had just returned from serving in Viet Nam with the Marine Corps. We met on a blind date and a year and a half later he had become my best friend and I married this Marine. I was surprised to find out I also married a hunter, a firefighter, an EMT, a mechanic, a missionary, a pastor but that story played out over a lifetime. We were fourteen years into our marriage when Tony and I found out who Jesus was. Finding Jesus was our personal Great Awakening.

> *Laura* — is one of the many Christians I met when I was searching for God. She was an amazing young teenager. I was a married woman with four children — a special relationship formed between us. We became kindred spirits from two different generations.

> *Rose* — desires a life of "Happily Ever After." She longs for a perfect marriage and a perfect family, but her hopes are dashed time after time. She is set free from the effects of emotional wounds and alcoholism as she meets Jesus. This was the beginning of hope. Mercy and goodness followed her now. The continuing process of deliverance takes time. Through the waiting,

Rose finds more of Father God for her life. She is healed from asthma attacks, and she sees more of Jesus in her life. She learns how to forgive and experiences freedom. She discovers there is more of the Holy Spirit than she ever imagined!

Steve and Beth—have experienced healing and deliverance. When Steve was a newborn, he had to undergo cancer treatments and he survived, but the treatment left him disfigured. Jesus the Healer had a timeline for Steve's healing. Thirty years later, Steve is married with three children and his wife, Beth, needs help from Jesus the Healer. Their story is amazing, but life seems too harsh to bear for a period of time. God has Steve and Beth in His sacred classroom.

They came to the understanding of three truths:
- God is for you, not against you.
- Jesus Christ takes you to deeper depths and higher heights than you could ever imagine.
- You get to choose whether or not you go with Him…our Creator gives us free will.

Christie—is an engineer by profession. She has a great job, a husband and two sons and doesn't need a thing in this world until the bottom drops out of her life. She reads the Bible for the first time and gets grounded in a healthy church. She and her sons discover what worship is. She learns what grace is and how to trust Jesus Christ. The Holy Spirit shows her what a biblical worldview looks like and surrounds Christie with Christian friends who walk her through devastation on every side, including financial ruin and the loss of a loved one.

Drew—was born into an ordinary family, but he was not an ordinary child. In his span of life, nineteen short years, his circle of influence numbered in the thousands. I called him my Angel Boy.

Evelyn — was born into revival, so she craves the Kingdom of God and His righteousness. Her mother died when she was nine years old, and she lost her father when she was twelve. Family members brought Evelyn into their home and raised her. As Evelyn raises six children of her own, she becomes an encourager to all who meet her. Her story is straight from her heart. Evelyn and her husband are shocked when one of their children reveals that he has chosen an alternate lifestyle. Her mother's heart aches whenever her beloved son takes another step farther away from his family. What is it about Evelyn that makes her resilient in adversity?

These testimonies are glimpses of saints who chose to put their faith in Jesus Christ. Each life is on the potter's wheel being intricately formed hour by hour, day by day until Jesus takes them home or until He comes again as He promised. These witnesses are not done yet. They are still fighting battles, still conquering through trials, and overcoming by the Blood of the Lamb and by the word of their testimony. As you read each story, ask yourself: Would God, the Creator of the universe, give **me** a new life? Can **I** hear His voice? Would He overshadow **me**? I hope you find Jesus in these pages, for He is your answer! Come and see if there is a God encounter for you under His shadow!

At the end of each chapter, you will find three sections that are discipleship tools:

> 1. Prayer Section — the ACTS model — Adoration, Confession, Thanksgiving, Supplication. This is learning to talk to God.
> 2. Process Section. With numerous thoughts bombarding our minds today, we need to sort and

quiet our thoughts and choose what we think about. We call that processing.

3. Biblical Worldview Section.

Every person has a worldview — it is their belief system. A worldview is a lens through which people view the world around them. Our worldview comes from personal experience, education, environment, religion, media, politics, culture, etc. A biblical worldview uses the Bible as the lens. A person with a biblical worldview has a belief system rooted in the Word of God, and he/she believes the Bible contains the truth to live by…absolute truth. The verses supplied in the Biblical Worldview Sections are not meant to be an exhaustive list. They are provided merely as a checklist for the reader. For example, angels are mentioned ninety-four times in ninety-two verses the King James Version. Check to see if what you believe lines up with the Word of God in the Biblical Worldview Sections following each chapter and in your own search.

In the Appendix Section, you will find Bible verses for references on various topics.

My heart's desire is for you to become a strong soldier in the Kingdom of God. I don't know how else to say it — you have to learn how to fight like a valiant well-trained soldier. You have to learn how to stand for Jesus. When you've done all, you're still standing and conquering. Quitting is not an option. Being lukewarm is not an option. If you begin this journey, you keep going forward. Here's a key: forget the things in your past and go forward. Surround yourself with people who have faith. I pray that you will mature in the knowledge of Jesus Christ as you read these pages. Now, let's go stir up our faith together!

Love to you,
Dianne Hall

Chapter One
Overshadowed by New Birth — Tony's Testimony

"Weird! Her behavior is weird, and I just don't get it." Tony muttered to himself as he walked in the back door of their house from a day at work. In just a few steps, he smelled a savory aroma and found his wife standing at the stove with earbuds on, listening intently while she prepared dinner. She was content. Happy as a lark.

"Hi, honey!" she says.

I'm grumbling to myself: "In the morning, in the evening, every time I see my wife, she's reading the Bible or listening to it on some device. We've been married for twelve years, and she has never done this before. What is going on? Why is she reading the Bible so much? She seems happy enough."

That very evening, I had a confrontation with Dianne in our living room. I stated firmly, "Our marriage is falling apart!" I said it while thinking it was her fault. How does she respond?

"Everything is wonderful!" She says as she wraps her arms around my neck and kisses me.

"Everything is going to be just fine."

That was the beginning of the change in my life. I didn't ask for change. I didn't want change. Change arrived unexpectedly like a dreadful tornado. I feared it would do damage. Nothing seemed "fine" about our situation. This storm had a mysterious force behind it. I wasn't able to discern what this was. I saw the decision I faced: I could bend with this force, or the force could break me into pieces. This was a force from another realm…it wasn't familiar at all.

A few weeks before I confronted Dianne, our neighbors invited her to go with them to this little country church up the road. I had no desire to go with her. Dianne came home and told me all about the sermon. She was so excited. The songs were inspiring her, and I believed her, but how can I accept these changes? I don't want her to take the kids with her to this church, and then I change my mind and tell her it's okay. The kids really like the church, too. Huh?

These changes occurred the year Dianne gave birth to our fourth child. She was experiencing Jesus and being drawn to Him by the Holy Spirit. Dianne recorded the songs that were so inspiring to her and played them in the labor and delivery room. As our baby arrived, the atmosphere in the room was peace and joy. We all felt it. The attending physician told us he really enjoyed the "spiritual" music. What was this music? Soft worship music with lyrics from the Bible.

Having a fourth child has changes of its own. We named our baby girl Elizabeth Ruth. Both her names come from the Hebrew language. "Elisheva," meaning "My God is abundance." Ruth means "companion, friend, and vision of beauty." Elizabeth was a tiny little bit of a thing, a vision of beauty with her big brown eyes and wispy blonde hair. She was a gift from God sent to us in His perfect timing. When she arrived, we had an abundance with two boys and two girls. Her birth coincided with our search for truth. God was beginning to make all things new for us.

I am grateful for that little country church and how Dianne was drawn to it. And that strange force I was unable to discern turned out to be the Holy Spirit. It wasn't long before I, too, responded to the Holy Spirit and made Jesus the Lord of my life. Having been raised Catholic, I felt secure that I knew God, but I was soon to find out that there was more to know who God is. Getting to know God involves a personal relationship with His Son Jesus Christ. As Dianne continued to visit the small country church during the fall season and share the sermons with me, I began to experience a spiritual tug-of-war between what she shared and what my Catholic upbringing taught me. She was learning what the Bible teaches. I could not deny anything she said. The winter season began, and I realized I needed to fully experience God. But how?

The evening of January 3, 1982, changed my life forever. I was at home with our four children, and Dianne was at the church for their Sunday evening service. Our children were tucked in for the night. I was having a time of reflection sitting in a chair in the living room. I didn't know it, but Dianne was at the altar praying for me. I remember very clearly feeling the Holy Spirit's prompting as I got down on my knees and said: "Lord, if all this change is You, I can't fight You. I invite you to come into my life, and I ask you to be my Savior, Jesus." With those few words, the tug-of-war ceased, and I had great peace. I knew Jesus was living inside me. My life was changed in a moment of time.

In the days and months following my salvation, I experienced a hunger for the Bible, and I understood what I read. I realized the transforming power of God comes from the Word of God. That is the reason our lives changed so much — God's overshadowing power drew us into the Word of God, and we wanted to know Him more. The Bible says that when we accept Christ, old things pass away, and all things become new. I finally understood what Dianne felt as she read her Bible.

Jesus became the center of our lives in our home and in our community. Prayer was our focus. I was a volunteer firefighter for thirteen years. I served from 1976 to 1989 and I remember those years as both challenging and unique times in our lives. What does the job of a volunteer firefighter entail? I was on call twenty-four sevens and training took place every Tuesday night. I joined the Bruce Township Fire Department, and we became like a close family. Our children never tired of going to the fire station. They were very proud of the fact their dad was a firefighter. At home, in our kitchen, we had a fire radio that sounded an alert and gave a description of the emergency. I also had a pager attached to my belt. I responded to the scene or drove to the fire station. Our children usually slept through the nighttime alerts. My coat and boots were ready and waiting for me to slip into and quickly jump into my pick-up truck. Dianne and I prayed for the firefighters and for all the

3

people involved in each rescue mission. The focus was all about serving people just like Jesus served people.

Ford Motor Company employed me as the cafeteria supervisor at the Romeo Tractor Plant. Ford permitted me to leave work and respond to a "run" (an emergency call) during the daytime hours as they considered it "Community Service." I became a "first responder" to tornado warnings, ice storms, house fires, traffic accidents, etc. On hectic days there were ambulance calls that required attention. Other times were quiet with no emergencies. Whether I responded to an emergency or stayed on the job depended on what I was required to do at work. I had a staff of twelve women and two men under my supervision. They saw the change in me right away after my encounter with Jesus. They had their own interpretation of what was going on in my life and whispered, "Tony's got religion."

One of the unexpected things God did at the beginning of our walk with Him was to set us free from alcohol. My wife and I were social drinkers. We had a liquor cabinet in our kitchen above the refrigerator. One of the items in the cabinet was a bottle of Seagram's Seven. This was the special kind of whiskey that came in a fancy blue bag with gold strings. I remembered these when I was growing up. Boys used the blue bags for their toy marbles. The bags were treasures. An acquaintance at work told me that he was regifting a bottle of whiskey to me because he didn't drink. He knew I did.

We went to a Bible Study on a Wednesday night, and this particular night the topic was alcohol. We went through every Bible verse that referenced "strong drink and wine." I remember walking out of the Bible Study with my wife that evening. As we exited through the church doors into the parking lot, I turned to her and asked, "Do you want to drink anymore?

She said, "No, do you?"

We heard the Word, and all desires for alcohol dropped off us like leaves falling in the autumn season. Would that change when we were with other people who were drinking? This was another occasion where we could see that God was overshadowing us. He had done the work—we didn't drink any longer. There was no desire in us to drink alcohol.

Our oldest daughter Laurie has a vivid childhood memory of an event that took place in our home. She remembers feeling surprised: "I walked into the kitchen one day to find my dad emptying the liquor cabinet which was over the refrigerator. He was pouring the contents of a glass bottle down the drain. When I asked, "Why?" Dad simply responded, "We don't need it anymore."

Laurie told us, "This event set an example for me that alcohol wasn't necessary to have fun. I've never had the desire to try it because my thought was: if my parents didn't need it, neither did I."

I had another significant life-changing experience when someone prophesied over my life for the first time. Because we were in the Catholic Charismatic Movement, we met many people. We arranged for a speaker to come to our church. Her name was Sister Loretta Melon. She was a powerhouse preacher of the Word of God and operated in the gifts of prophecy and healing.

I will never forget how one minute Sister Loretta was preaching, and the next minute she was standing right in front of me prophesying. "Oh, brother," she said, "If you will get into My Word, says the Lord, I have marvelous things for you."

This was a powerful experience for me. I did get into God's Word, and the journey the Lord took me and my family on has been powerful, too. The prophecy was the beginning of God working in our lives with prophetic gifts given by the Holy Spirit. We believed in the laying on of hands, prophecy, and all the gifts of the Holy Spirit because we experienced them.

Today, my wife and I continue to be involved in rescue missions, but they have taken on a different form. Rescue work in the natural lives of people is very much like rescue work in their spiritual lives. Jesus invites us to go out into the highways and byways and compel people to come into the Kingdom of God — these are spiritual rescue missions. As we pray and testify, people come to know Jesus Christ as their Savior. We see God overshadow them. They get healed, set-free, and find the Bible for the first time in their lives. They learn how to pray and invite God to intervene in their circumstances. God uses whoever is willing to be active in His Kingdom. Active is the key word. Faith is action. Praying for people is action.

We remembered a significant event that took place at Bethlehem Ephratah church where we served many years ago. We always had a time of prayer at the altar following our services. A friend of ours who was nine months pregnant came to the altar for prayer because her baby was in the breech position. We laid hands on her, and all of a sudden, we saw movement in her womb that we have never encountered since. Her baby moved out of a breech position, and we saw it! We were all amazed at the power of God. Her son was born a few days later with a normal childbirth. This is the God we serve!

So here I am, forty years later, loving life with Jesus. Over these years, I have had the privilege of serving as a deacon, elder, missionary, and the last fourteen years as a pastor, serving in pastoral care. I look forward to the journey that lies ahead of us as we walk together in service with our Lord and Savior Jesus Christ. We received another prophecy over our lives that we see unfolding today, and we know the best is yet to come.

What is a Testimony?

Tony has just written his "testimony." It's a story of how his life changed when Jesus Christ came and revealed Himself to Tony. Life was never the same after that.

A simple definition for a testimony is a formal written or spoken statement, especially one given in a court of law. A Christian testimony is a written or spoken statement declaring that Jesus Christ has changed a person's life. The Bible tells us that our testimony is life to others. Our testimony is a spiritual weapon and by our testimony we overcome the evil around us. We are in a spiritual war, and we have an enemy that does not want us to succeed in any way.

Let's look at a very important verse from the Book of Revelation that we need to understand:

They triumphed over him by the blood of the Lamb and by the word of their testimony; they did not love their lives so much as to shrink from death.
Revelation 12:11 (NIV)

When we read Revelation 12:11, we learn that the Blood of Jesus has power, and it gives us victory, but to whom is this verse referring? Who are "they?" Who is "him?" How are "they" triumphing over? What is the word of a testimony?

The verse refers to the people of God as "they." The people of God triumphed. That's us! "Him" is referencing Satan. The people of God triumphed over Satan. That's great news! How did the people of God triumph over Satan?

1) By the blood of the Lamb.
2) By the word of their testimony.

When we study the Bible, one way to get a clearer picture of a verse we may be grappling with is to look at other Bible versions. Above, we have used the NIV.

We have noted the "who:" believers and Satan;

the "what:" the blood of the Lamb and our testimony.

"Where:" is on earth.

"When:" is whenever Satan attacks.

Below, we will set up a comparison to four other versions of the Bible and look more closely at the "action words" and the "how."

The English Standard Version ESV — *And they <u>have conquered him</u> by the blood of the Lamb and <u>by the word of their testimony,</u> for they loved not their lives even unto death.*

The Good News translation GNT — They <u>won the victory over him</u> by the blood of the Lamb and <u>by the truth which they proclaimed</u>; and they were willing to give up their lives and die.

The Message Bible MSG — They <u>defeated him</u> through the blood of the Lamb and <u>the bold word of their witness</u>. They weren't in love with themselves; they were willing to die for Christ.

The Complete Jewish Bible CJB — They <u>defeated him</u> because of the Lamb's blood and because of <u>the message of their witness.</u> Even when facing death they did not cling to life.

Let's look at the action:	Let's find out how the people overcame Satan:
The people of God triumphed over him (Satan)	By the blood of the lamb and the word of their testimony
The people of God have conquered him (Satan)	by the blood of the Lamb and the word of their testimony.
The people of God won the victory over him (Satan)	by the blood of the Lamb and by the truth they proclaimed
The people of God won victory over him (Satan)	by the blood of the Lamb and by the truth they proclaimed
The people of God defeated him (Satan)	through the blood of the Lamb and the bold word of their witness
The people of God defeated him (Satan)	because of the Lamb's blood and because of the message of their witness

It is of interest that the Greek word for "testimony" is martyria (transliterates), similar to our English word "martyr." When we focus on the second part of Revelation 12:11 and compare the different versions, we learn how "testimony" links to the word "martyr:"

- — they did not love their lives so much as to shrink from death. (NIV)
- — for they loved not their lives even unto death. (ESV)
- — and they were willing to give up their lives and die. (GNT)
- — They weren't in love with themselves; they were willing to die for Christ. (MSG)
- — Even when facing death, they did not cling to life. (CJB)

When Jesus died on the cross, Satan was defeated. We cannot overcome Satan on our own. Our power comes from Jesus' completed work on earth when He shed His blood on the cross. Jesus is referred to as the Lamb of God. Jesus is THE sacrifice for sins.

What were Jesus' last words on the cross?

When he had received the drink, Jesus said, "It is finished." With that, he bowed his head and gave up his spirit.
John 19:30 (NIV)

Jesus' work is finished. He sits at the right hand of God. Our work on earth has begun. Our testimony of how Jesus has changed our lives is life to others.

We have been given everything we need to overcome whatever this life brings our way and witness the life we have in Jesus Christ. God gave us His Son. God gave us His Word. We have the armor of God. We have the Blood of Jesus. We have the Holy Spirit. God overshadows us with grace and mercy. Let's be about the Father's business just like Jesus did when He was on the earth. Jesus has ordained us to do the Father's Kingdom work!

Overshadowed by New Birth — Tony's Testimony

ACTS Prayer

At the end of every chapter, we will use the ACTS model for prayer. Prayer is humbly talking to God. We adore, confess, give thanks, and intercede for others using the Word of God. Write your prayers in the spaces provided. If you are in a group study, keep the confessions of others confidential. You do not have to share out loud, but the Holy Spirit may lead you to share your experience with the group. There may be someone in your group study that needs to hear what you have to say. Let the Holy Spirit lead you.

A is for adoration. We enter God's Presence adoring and praising Him. He loves us.

C is for confession. We confess and repent of any sin the Holy Spirit reveals to us.

T is for thanksgiving. There is always something to be thankful for!

S is for supplication. We petition God for the things we and others need.

Worship Jesus as the Rock of your Salvation

Adoration: We honor you as Jesus the Rock of our Salvation.

Lord Jesus, I worship you for coming after me, for pursuing me. You have been so good to me. I adore you for creating me and bringing me to really a place where I see who You are — the lover of my soul, my Savior, my Lord, the Rock of my salvation.

Confession: I confess that I thought my life was okay without You, Jesus. I didn't seek you out. You sought me. I will trust in you, forever, for you are the Rock eternal.

Thanksgiving: I thank You that you didn't let me stay in my unbelief. You rescued me from a life void of You, Jesus. My life is so much richer because You are in my life. Thank you for rescuing me from death and giving me life.

Supplication: I call to you from the ends of the earth, I call as my heart grows faint; lead me to the rock that is higher than I. I pray that my classmates, my family, my work associates, and every person I come in contact with will find You, Father, and that each one would come to the saving knowledge of Jesus Christ and what He did for us on the cross.

Overshadowed by New Birth — Tony's Testimony

Process What You Have Learned

To process means to think about what you are thinking about. Have you noticed that we get so busy we don't even have time to think? You can process with a cup of coffee and take a mini vacation. At the end of every chapter, these pages are to help you slow down and meditate on what you have just read. You may have experienced a new revelation from God while reading. You can write the revelation in these spaces. You want to write down when God speaks to your heart.

1. Did you grow up reading the Bible? Were you raised in a certain denomination?

2. Could you relate to Tony's story about a tug-of-war in things you were taught about God?

3. Is the Holy Spirit speaking to you to enter into a closer relationship with the Father?

   With Jesus?

4. Can God change your heart? Will God go against your free will?

5. Alcohol causes so much suffering in families today. Has alcohol been a part of your life?

Overshadowed by New Birth — Tony's Testimony

Biblical Worldview of Salvation in Jesus Christ

Biblical References

Word of God — The Bible is the Word of God and more than just a book. We call it the Holy Bible. Proverbs 30:5; Isaiah 40:8; Jeremiah 15:16; Matthew 4:4; Mark 7:13; Luke 8:11; Luke 11:28; Acts 4:31; Acts 6:7; Acts 12:24

> *For the Word of God is living and active, sharper than any two-edged sword, piercing to the division of soul and of spirit, of joints and of marrow, and discerning the thoughts and intentions of the heart.*
> Hebrews 4:12 (ESV)

Jesus is the Only Way to God — The Bible tells us Jesus Christ is the only way to God. When people say there are many ways to God, this is not biblical. If there are other ways to God, then Jesus' sacrifice would have no value. His death on the cross would be in vain. John 8:24; Acts 4:12

> *Jesus said to him, "I am the [only] Way [to God] and the [real] Truth and the [real] Life; no one comes to the Father but through Me."*
> John 14:6 (AMP)

> *How much greater punishment do you think he will deserve who has rejected and trampled under foot the Son of God, and has considered unclean and common the blood of the covenant that sanctified him, and has insulted the Spirit of grace [who imparts the unmerited favor and blessing of God]?*
> Hebrews 10:29 (AMP)

Salvation — Luke 1:71; Luke 1:77; Luke 2:30; Luke 3:6

> *And He has raised up a horn of salvation [a mighty and valiant Savior] for us In the house of David His servant —*
> Luke 1:69 (AMP)

14

Jesus said to him, "Today salvation has come to this household, because he, too, is a [spiritual] son of Abraham;
Luke 19:9 (AMP)

"Brothers, sons of Abraham's family, and those among you who fear God, to us has been sent the message of this salvation [obtained through faith in Jesus Christ].
Acts 13:26 (AMP)

Salvation for the Gentiles — Acts 13:47; Isaiah 11:10; Isaiah 42:1; Isaiah 49:6; Matthew 12:21; Acts 10:45; Acts 11:18; Acts 13:46, 48; Acts 14:27; Acts 18:6

"Therefore let it be known to you that [this message of] the salvation of God has been sent to the Gentiles; they indeed will listen!"
Acts 28:28 (AMP)

Forgiveness of Sins — Jesus is the atonement for sin. Colossians 1:14; Acts 13:38; Acts 26:18; Ephesians 1:7

But if you do not forgive others [nurturing your hurt and anger with the result that it interferes with your relationship with God], then your Father will not forgive your trespasses.
Matthew 6:15 (AMP)

Our Deliverance from Sin

But if we walk in the light as He is in the light, we have fellowship with one another, and the blood of Jesus Christ His Son cleanses us from all sin. If we say that we have no sin, we deceive ourselves, and the truth is not in us. If we confess our sins, He is faithful and just to forgive us our sins and to cleanse us from all unrighteousness.
1 John 1:7-9 (NKJV)

Other gods - Idolatry — When people say we all worship the same God, this is not biblical. There are many gods — small "g." The worship of other gods is idolatry. Exodus 12:12; Exodus 32:1; Judges 2:12; Psalm 40:4; Jeremiah 16:19; Psalm 4:2; Acts 7:40

> *"You shall not make for yourself any idol, or any likeness (form, manifestation) of what is in heaven above or on the earth beneath or in the water under the earth [as an object to worship]. ...You shall not worship them nor serve them; for I, the Lord your God, am a jealous (impassioned) God [demanding what is rightfully and uniquely mine], visiting (avenging) the iniquity (sin, guilt) of the fathers on the children [that is, calling the children to account for the sins of their fathers], to the third and fourth generations of those who hate Me, ...but showing graciousness and steadfast lovingkindness to thousands [of generations] of those who love Me and keep My commandments.*
> Exodus 20:4-6 (AMP)

> *They even sacrificed their sons and their daughters to demons.*
> Psalm 106:37 (AMP)

Jesus Came to Fulfill the Law and to Establish a New Covenant — 1 Corinthians 11:25; 2 Corinthians 3:6

> *"Do not think that I have come to do away with or undo the Law [of Moses] or the [writings of the] Prophets; I did not come to destroy but to fulfill.*
> Matthew 5:17 (AMP)

> *And in the same way He took the cup after they had eaten, saying, "This cup, which is poured out for you, is the new covenant [ratified] in My blood.*
> Luke 22:20 (AMP)

For this reason He is the Mediator and Negotiator of a new covenant [that is, an entirely new agreement uniting God and man], so that those who have been called [by God] may receive [the fulfillment of] the promised eternal inheritance, since a death has taken place [as the payment] which redeems them from the sins committed under the obsolete first covenant.
Hebrews 9:15 (AMP)

Overshadowed by New Birth — Tony's Testimony

Biblical Worldview of Alcohol (Wine and Strong Drink)

Biblical References

Drunkenness — is first mentioned in Genesis — it brought a curse. Genesis 19:32-35; Proverbs 26:9; Psalm 107:27

> *And Noah began to farm and cultivate the ground and he planted a vineyard. …He drank some of the wine and became drunk, and he was uncovered and lay exposed inside his tent.*
> Genesis 9:20-21 (AMP)

> *Let us behave decently, as in the daytime, not in carousing and drunkenness, not in sexual immorality and debauchery, not in dissension and jealousy.*
> Romans 13:13 (NIV)

Wine — can be fermented or unfermented. When we search the Scriptures, we look at the root meaning of the words to determine what a passage says. Examples:

Hebrew words: yayin (fermented), tirosh (fresh juice or new wine), shakar (drunk)

Greek words: oinos (wine), methysko (get drunk), pino (drink), oinopotes (drunkard)

> *"Do not drink wine or intoxicating drink, neither you nor your sons with you, when you come into the Tent of Meeting, so that you will not die — it is a permanent statute throughout your generations —*
> Leviticus 10:9 (AMP)

> *Wine is a mocker, strong drink a riotous brawler; and whoever is intoxicated by it is not wise.*
> Proverbs 20:1 (AMP)

Woes [Judgments] — are associated with alcohol — Proverbs 23:29-35; Proverbs 31:7; Isaiah 5:20-23

> *Listen, my son, and be wise, And direct your heart in the way [of the Lord]. ...Do not associate with heavy drinkers of wine, Or with gluttonous eaters of meat, ...For the heavy drinker and the glutton will come to poverty, And the drowsiness [of overindulgence] will clothe one with rags.*
> Proverbs 23:19-21 (AMP)

> *Woe (judgment is coming) to those who rise early in the morning to pursue intoxicating drink, Who stay up late in the night till wine inflames them!... They have lyre and harp, tambourine and flute, and wine at their feasts; But they do not regard nor even pay attention to the deeds of the Lord, Nor do they consider the work of His hands.*
> Isaiah 5:11-12 (AMP)

> *"Woe (judgment is coming) to you who make your neighbors drink, Who mix in your venom to make them drunk So that you may look at their nakedness!*
> Habakkuk 2:15 (AMP)

The Apostle Paul Tells Us Plainly What Sin Is — drunkenness is among other sins. Galatians 5:19-21; Peter explains: 1 Peter 4:1-6; Jesus explains: Matthew 24:45-51; Luke 7:33-35; Mark 15:23

> *But actually, I have written to you not to associate with any so-called [Christian] brother if he is sexually immoral or greedy, or is an idolater [devoted to anything that takes the place of God], or is a reviler [who insults or slanders or otherwise verbally abuses others], or is a drunkard or a swindler — you must not so much as eat with such a person.*
> 1 Corinthians 5:11 (AMP)

19

Notice in these verses above that the Apostle Paul explains that Christians (believers) should not walk in the sins mentioned. They have been redeemed, and their lives show that. Below, the text names the sin of the unrighteous and states, "such were some of you." Paul reminds the believers that they were "washed, sanctified (made holy), and justified." They have changed lives because of the sacrifice of Jesus and the work of the Holy Spirit. Look and consider this list. It is a simple fact — we have all sinned and come short of the glory of God. When Jesus saves us, we walk away from those sins. The power of God changes us. The righteousness of Jesus covers us.

> *Do you not know that the unrighteous will not inherit or have any share in the kingdom of God? Do not be deceived; neither the sexually immoral, nor idolaters, nor adulterers, nor effeminate [by perversion], nor those who participate in homosexuality,...nor thieves, nor the greedy, nor drunkards, nor revilers [whose words are used as weapons to abuse, insult, humiliate, intimidate, or slander], nor swindlers will inherit or have any share in the kingdom of God. ...And such were some of you [before you believed]. But you were washed [by the atoning sacrifice of Christ], you were sanctified [set apart for God, and made holy], you were justified [declared free of guilt] in the name of the Lord Jesus Christ and in the [Holy] Spirit of our God [the source of the believer's new life and changed behavior].*
> 1 Corinthians 6:9-11 (AMP)

> *Be very careful, then, how you live — not as unwise but as wise, making the most of every opportunity, because the days are evil. Therefore do not be foolish, but understand what the Lord's will is. Do not get drunk on wine, which leads to debauchery. Instead, be filled with the Spirit.*
> Ephesians 5:15-18 (NIV)

"Be careful, or your hearts will be weighed down with carousing, drunkenness and the anxieties of life, and that day will close on you suddenly like a trap. For it will come on all those who live on the face of the whole earth. Be always on the watch, and pray that you may be able to escape all that is about to happen, and that you may be able to stand before the Son of Man."
Luke 21:34-36 (NIV)

Our Deliverance from Sin

But if we walk in the light as He is in the light, we have fellowship with one another, and the blood of Jesus Christ His Son cleanses us from all sin. If we say that we have no sin, we deceive ourselves, and the truth is not in us. If we confess our sins, He is faithful and just to forgive us our sins and to cleanse us from all unrighteousness.
1 John 1:7-9 (NKJV)

John the Baptist — What is a Nazarite vow? — Samson mentioned in Judges 13:7

[The angel announced to Zechariah] He [John the Baptist] will be a joy and delight to you, and many will rejoice because of his birth, ...for he will be great in the sight of the Lord. He is never to take wine or other fermented drink, and he will be filled with the Holy Spirit even before he is born. ...He will bring back many of the people of Israel to the Lord their God. ...And he will go on before the Lord, in the spirit and power of Elijah, to turn the hearts of the parents to their children and the disobedient to the wisdom of the righteous — to make ready a people prepared for the Lord."
Luke 1:14-17 (NIV)

What is a Nazarite Vow?

The Bible explains what a Nazarite is in the Book of Numbers. When a person wanted to dedicate their lives to God, they took a Nazarite vow.

Then the Lord spoke to Moses, saying, ..."Speak to the children of Israel, and say to them: 'When either a man or woman consecrates an offering to take the vow of a Nazirite, to separate himself to the Lord, ...he shall separate himself from wine and similar drink; he shall drink neither vinegar made from wine nor vinegar made from similar drink; neither shall he drink any grape juice, nor eat fresh grapes or raisins. ...All the days of his separation he shall eat nothing that is produced by the grapevine, from seed to skin. ...'All the days of the vow of his separation no razor shall come upon his head; until the days are fulfilled for which he separated himself to the Lord, he shall be holy. Then he shall let the locks of the hair of his head grow. ...All the days that he separates himself to the Lord he shall not go near a dead body. ...He shall not make himself unclean even for his father or his mother, for his brother or his sister, when they die, because his separation to God is on his head. ...All the days of his separation he shall be holy to the Lord.
Numbers 6:1-8 (NKJV)

Wine not for Kings or Leaders, Overseers, Bishops, Elders, Deacons — Ecclesiastes 10:17; Daniel 1:8; 1 Timothy 3:1-7; Titus 1:7; Titus 2:3

It is not for kings, Lemuel – it is not for kings to drink wine, not for rulers to crave beer, lest they drink and forget what has been decreed, and deprive all the oppressed of their rights.
Proverbs 31:4-5 (NIV)

In the same way, deacons are to be worthy of respect, sincere, not indulging in much wine, and not pursuing dishonest gain. They must keep hold of the deep truths of the faith with a clear conscience. They must first be tested; and then if there is nothing against them, let them serve as deacons.
1 Timothy 1:9-10 (NIV)

Chapter Two

Overshadowed by God's Comfort — Dianne's Testimony

On a hot summer morning, July 28th, to be exact, a head-on collision occurred on the two-lane highway near our home. Within minutes, sirens blared — the rescuers were on the scene quickly. The loud cutting sound of the Jaws-of-Life tool broke the early morning stillness, and with great care, they removed the body of a young woman from her vehicle. The rescuers found that her vital signs were gone. Her youth was extinguished in a matter of seconds when one of the cars crossed over the middle line as she drove to work.

Five Years Earlier

When I was around thirty years of age, if you had asked me what I thought about God, I would have said I knew God, and I knew Jesus was His Son who died on a cross for our sins. I would have told you that I had a reverence for God. I prayed daily. I would have also told you that God seemed to be a faraway entity to me — He was out there somewhere. My concept of a distant God was about to change forever. Almighty God unmasked Himself to me. He came to me using people from every generation: Pastor Carl Halquist and his wife, Sandy, who had high school-age children; our neighbors, John and Donna who had married children and grandchildren; Tom and Sharon, the leaders of our Charismatic Bible Study/Prayer Group, a young couple our age; Dolores, a woman who worked for Tony, married with older children. God provided incredible people for our journey.

I volunteered to teach the eighth-grade catechism class at St. Clement of Rome Catholic Church. Teaching this class was a challenge for me because I was a stay-at-home mom consumed with raising our four children. I was called to be the teacher, but I was going to become the student.

One of my students was a young teen named Laura. When Laura told me that she was in a youth group at another church, I was fascinated. I thought you couldn't do that. You know, it would be against the rules to go to two churches at the same time, and not only that, the churches were two different denominations. Oh, now that's really against the rules. Isn't it? I could see Laura was walking out her faith in God in her everyday life. The godly qualities I observed in her life tugged at my heart. I began to realize I was searching for something. I didn't know what I was searching for. If I believed I knew God, then it wasn't God I was searching for.

I had questions about life; Laura had answers.

I had doubts; Laura had faith in God.

I was unsure; Laura had confidence.

Laura's heart was alive…my heart was struggling.

Laura had a personal relationship with Jesus, and I did not know how to get close to Jesus.

It wasn't "something" I needed; it was "Someone." Simply put: I needed Jesus Christ. Laura was a blessing sent from God for me. I met her at a time when I was feeling an emptiness. The emptiness that I was feeling made me ask myself: "What's this life about anyway?" I pondered that question as I sat on our lawn tractor mowing up and down, back and forth, covering our 1.7 acres of land. The Holy Spirit was drawing me. This drawing was happening in a supernatural realm I didn't know anything about. I decided I wanted more of God. Decision. Every person has a decision to make. We choose God or reject God.

I was religious and judgmental. My strong religious ways had to crumble. I needed truth. Only the Holy Spirit would be able to convince me I needed change in my life. Only He could show me that Jesus is the way, the truth, and the life.

One yearning led to another, and I found myself going to two churches. I became a rule-breaker, but I couldn't help myself! I was hungry and thirsty for more of God. Jesus is the way, the truth, and the life, and He's the only one who can lead us to His Father. The Hobbs were neighbor friends who used to attend with us at St. Clement of Rome Church. They invited me to the little country church they were attending called Maranatha Assembly of God. Quite coincidentally, Laura and her family attended here. I started to take my children with me and was pleasantly surprised to find they loved the Bible classes and games. The adults studied the Bible in the sanctuary. Wednesday nights were referred to as the mid-week service and Family Night. This was new to me. I had not heard of a "mid-week" service. I used to go to Novenas to Mary, the mother of Jesus, on Tuesday nights with my dad, but this was different.

I was learning about Jesus living on the earth and what He did when He was here. (He's a historical figure, just in case you are doubting Jesus is a real person.) His feet walked in the earth's dust from town to town. He drank water from a well. Everywhere He went, He healed people. I was learning that Jesus was coming to earth again! I didn't know what the Bible said about that. This was new to me, too! New people, new songs, new gifts, new birth.

Then, something happened! I went to this small country church on a Sunday morning. The pastor asked all the people who needed healing to come to the front of the church for prayer. I had a skin condition called psoriasis. I believed in healing. Nothing could have stopped me from going forward. I felt like my legs were running to the altar on their own. When the pastor put his hand on my head to pray over me, I heard myself saying out of my innermost being, my spirit: "I accept you as my Savior, Jesus." Jesus changed my heart forever in an instant!

After that service, I began to read and understand what the Bible said. My questions were being answered. That is how I got close to Jesus. God used Laura to lead me to hear the Gospel. The day was November 8. God overshadowed me, and I experienced new life in Jesus Christ!

I visited my parents just after Christmas, and I can remember sitting on the floor at my dad's feet. I was so excited to share what was going on inside of me. I told Dad how I was reading the Bible, and that I had this wonderful "Born Again Experience." My dad was the one who taught me how to pray each night before bed. He was the one who made sure we went to church every Sunday. It wasn't at all unusual that I wanted to tell Dad most of all. He didn't really say much. I wish he would have bared his heart with me that day. He just listened to me and nodded. Mom sent a letter to me the next week and said: "We loved your visit. Dad says he doesn't need to be 'born again' in order to know His Savior." At first, I was disheartened. The Bible says we need to be "born again." I didn't understand, but the Holy Spirit showed me the truth: my dad believed Jesus was his Savior.

Then Jesus cried out, "Whoever believes in me does not believe in me only, but in the one who sent me."
John 12:44 (NIV)

My visit between Christmas and New Year's Day was the last time I saw my dad alive. In March, my dad died during a minor surgical procedure. He had a weak heart, and the surgery caused stress on his heart. When I heard the news of his death, I kept saying, "But I wasn't there with him." I became very thankful for that last visit with my dad. I knew he loved me, and I knew he loved God. I felt like I was handed a baton of prayer from my dad. Dad prayed, taught me how to pray, and now I was to continue to pray for our family and all our future generations that they would know Jesus Christ as their Savior. My dad left me a godly heritage. God cares about every generation, and He tells us in His Word:

For the Lord is good and his love endures forever; his faithfulness continues through all generations.
Psalm 100:5 (NIV)

When I returned home from my visit with Dad and Mom, I left the kids with Tony and headed to the Sunday night service at church. I still had lots of questions about this new life. The pastor made an invitation to come to the altar to receive the Holy Spirit. I wanted everything that God wanted to give me, so I went down to the altar. I was filled with the Baptism of the Holy Spirit with the evidence of speaking in tongues. Then, I prayed for my husband, Tony. When I turned around, I saw only the pastor and his wife praying with me, the rest of the people had gone home. It was nine o'clock, and I had been at church for three hours! With Tony at home with our four kids, I felt the need to get home as quickly as possible. All was peaceful when I arrived home.

The following Thursday, Tony and I were on our way to the Charismatic Bible Study at Tom and Sharon's home. We pulled up the driveway. Tony turned off the ignition, turned to me, and said:

"They can welcome a new brother in Christ at the study tonight. I asked Jesus into my heart Sunday night while you were at church!" I could hear the excitement in his voice.

Then, it was my turn to share with Tony: "I received the Holy Spirit baptism with the evidence of speaking in tongues last Sunday night at church!"

I cannot tell you why we waited four days to speak to each other about these amazing events.

We exited the car, walked to the front door, knocked on the door, and together we shared with our friends in Home Group the marvelous things God was doing in our lives. This was the beginning of our ministering together as a team. We learned so much in our first Bible study, and we have Tom and Sharon to thank for all that they poured into our lives back then.

The next few years were spent raising our children, enjoying our life in the country, and learning all we could about living for Jesus. We loved living in Romeo, Michigan. Our entire family was involved in the community. Tony was coaching baseball for our son Chris' team. Laurie and I were involved with Indian Maidens, a mother-daughter program through the YMCA. Our two little toddlers, Jason and

Elizabeth, were growing like sunflowers — tall and quick. Tony was working at Ford Motor Company. He was also responding to emergency calls as a volunteer firefighter. Our lives were busy and full.

There was one particular emergency call we were not prepared for. The tragic day came during the summer on July 28. Tony was not on duty that day. We heard about a head-on collision on the highway near our home, and we were shocked to discover the young woman was our friend Laura. I was heartbroken. My father's death did not have the pain or impact Laura's death had on me. Laura was so young, and the news had a jarring effect on her family and friends, on my family, and the youth group at the church. When there is a person's tragic death, we need God's comfort as we deal with the overwhelming shock. Thoughts begin racing through our minds: Why did this happen? Does God care about these stunning blows that life inflicts on us suddenly? I knew God cared. I had no doubts about that, but there was a strong sense of sorrow of immense proportions in my heart.

The reality of life is: we do not know how many days we have on this earth. The Bible had answers for me as I read:

Teach us to number our days, that we may gain a heart of wisdom.
Psalm 90:12 (NIV)

Jesus promised:

Blessed are those who mourn, for they shall be comforted.
Matthew 5:4 (NKJV)

This is what I know. Laura was actively pursuing her relationship with Jesus. We did not know how many days she had on this earth. At Laura's funeral, the Lord introduced me to a beloved hymn called: "It Is Well with My Soul," I didn't grow up knowing hymns, and I had not heard this one before. I still remember Laura's funeral. I recall the mixed feelings I had: numbness...sorrow...shock. To this day, I think of Laura when I hear this hymn. I went home from the funeral that day, sat down, and wrote out the words. I placed the lyrics in my wallet. I didn't want to forget how comforted I felt by this song. Why would I be comforted? Worship. We worshiped on earth that day, and we joined Laura in the worship going on in heaven. I received comfort for my grief. God uses funeral services, songs, hymns, people to comfort us when we have losses.

We are connected to our brothers and sisters in Christ even when they have gone to heaven before us. In that holy place of worship, God comforted me. The Lord is always at work drawing us to Himself, and He drew me that day. I met Him as the "God of all comfort," and it produced in me compassion to comfort others.

Worship is a time when we can feel God's Presence. The soul consists of the mind, the will, and the emotions. Through Jesus, our mind, will, and emotions can be well!

I have included a portion of the lyrics. I encourage you to read the dramatic story behind this revered hymn in Appendix Two. You will also find the lyrics in their entire form.

1873 Hymn

It Is Well with My Soul by Horatio Spafford

When peace like a river, attendeth my way,
When sorrows like sea billows roll;
Whatever my lot, Thou hast taught me to say
It is well, it is well, with my soul

Refrain: It is well, (it is well),
With my soul (with my soul)
It is well, it is well with my soul

Though Satan should buffet, though trials should come,
Let this blest assurance control,
That Christ has regarded my helpless estate,
And hath shed His own blood for my soul

Refrain

My sin, oh, the bliss of this glorious thought!
My sin, not in part but the whole,
Is nailed to the cross, and I bear it no more,
Praise the Lord, praise the Lord, O my soul!

Refrain

Anna Spafford and her four daughters traveled on a French ocean liner from America to Europe in 1873. Her husband, Horatio Spafford, was planning to join the family later after he attended to pressing business matters. The ship that carried Anna and her daughters was named the *S.S. Ville du Havre*. In the middle of the night, their ship collided with another ship. The passenger liner sank within twelve minutes, taking the lives of an estimated 226 passengers. Distressed, Anna sent a message to her husband with devastating news: "*Saved but saved alone. What shall I do?*" All four of their daughters perished.

Horatio Spafford boarded a ship to sail to his grieving wife. During the voyage, the captain invited Horatio to his cabin and explained that he had calculated the spot where the ship had gone down. He let Horatio know that they were, at that moment, passing over the very spot. Horatio went to his cabin and wrote the words for the hymn "It Is Well With My Soul."

There are times when someone else's story gives us the hope we need in our dire circumstances. I found that hope in the words of this hymn and the sad story behind the hymn. Are you mourning? Have you had a loss in your life? Many losses? Losses come in many forms: the death of a loved one, losing a job or a friend; not receiving a promotion; moving away from friends and family; having a miscarriage. These are all losses. Knowing that someone survived a heartbreaking tragedy births hope in us. That's the power of Horatio and Anna Spafford's testimony.

The beautiful truth in the third stanza touched my heart. Jesus' sacrifice on the cross took the punishment for my sins. I feel joy and exhilaration when I read it—I am washed clean! My sin, oh, the bliss of this glorious thought My sin, not
in part but the whole,
Is nailed to the cross, and I bear it no more,
It is well, it is well with my soul.

Have you invited Jesus Christ to come and live inside of you? You might be saying to yourself, Jesus would not accept me—I have lived a bad life. The Good News is He waits for you to come to Him! He loves you! The Bible says:

> Here I am! I stand at the door and knock. If anyone hears my voice and opens the door, I will come in and eat with that person, and they with me.
> Revelation 3:20 (NIV)

Jesus is standing at the door of your heart. He is knocking. Will you open the door to Him? He is outside asking anyone who hears His voice to invite Him in. I encourage you to open the door of your heart and make room for Jesus. God has mercy and forgiveness of sins for you. God wants to give you a new life. You can get right with God at this very moment. If you desire to have a new life, I invite you to pray this prayer from your heart:

> Lord Jesus, I open the door. Please come in. I ask you to live inside my heart. I give you my life today. Thank you for dying for my sins. I receive your new life. I want to be changed into your image and likeness. Thank you for loving me. Thank you for forgiving all my sins. I am washed. I am clean by the blood you shed for me on the cross. Show me how to live this life with You as my Lord and Savior. Open up your Word to me. I ask all this in the Name of Jesus Christ. Amen.

_____Write today's date here. This is the day your new life begins!

31

Overshadowed by God's Comfort — Dianne's Testimony

ACTS Prayer

Worship God as your Comforter

Adoration: Father, I love you. I love that you comfort me, and I know that I'm not alone in this world. I worship you for the people around me who are in my life. I see Your hand in my life, and I praise you. I pray that I will be a vessel of comfort for others because of how you comfort me.

Confession: Lord, forgive me for not appreciating the people in my life. I want that to change. I see now you have given me people for my life—family, friends, work associates, all ages. Show me how to tell them about You. Help me speak when someone around me needs comforting.

Thanksgiving: Thank you for giving me people and songs for my life. I thank you for people younger and older than I am. Thank you to my family and all my relatives; each one is valuable. Thank you for helping me appreciate what you have made. Thank you for answering my prayers.

Supplication: You are my comfort in sorrow; my heart is faint within me. Comfort those around me, Lord. Many are feeling a loss. I bring before you my family, friends, and work associates that they would receive salvation. I want to be a light that shines in the darkness, Lord. I ask you to help me open my Bible every day. I ask you to reveal truths to me that I might not be aware of.

Overshadowed by God's Comfort — Dianne's Testimony

Process What You Have Learned

1. What was missing from Dianne's life? Is there something missing in your life?

2. What fruit did Laura's life exhibit?

3. Do you have a person from a different generation in your life who could bring you a different perspective? Older, younger? Is there more than one person?

4. Have you ever heard a song or songs that influenced your life? Name them.

   Do you have a favorite song that takes you into the Lord's Presence?

5. Look up Romans 5:12-20. Death in Adam, Life in Jesus. Discuss.

Overshadowed by God's Comfort — Dianne's Testimony

The Biblical Worldview on Death

Biblical References

Death — There are three types of death: spiritual death, physical death, eternal death. Proverbs 14:32; Ecclesiastes 7:1; 1 Corinthians 15:26; 1 Corinthians 15:55; Revelation 14:13; Psalm 23:4

> *There is a time for everything, and a season for every activity under the heavens: ...a time to be born and a time to die, a time to plant and a time to uproot.*
> Ecclesiastes 3:1-2 (NIV)

> *Why, you do not even know what will happen tomorrow. What is your life? You are a mist that appears for a while and then vanishes.*
> James 4:14 (NIV)

Jesus and Adam — When Adam disobeyed God, sin entered the world, and death came through sin. Because Jesus obeyed God, in Christ all become alive. Jesus was without sin. 1 Corinthians 15:44-49

> *For as in Adam all die, so in Christ all will be made alive.*
> 1 Corinthians 15:22 (NIV)

> *Therefore, just as sin entered the world through one man, and death through sin, and in this way death came to all people, because all sinned —*
> Romans 5:12 (NIV)

God Cares About Us in Death — Romans 5:10,12,14,17,21; Romans 6:23; Revelation 14:13

> *Precious in the sight of the Lord is the death of His saints.*
> Psalm 116:15 (NKJV)

I consider that our present sufferings are not worth comparing with the glory that will be revealed in us.
Romans 8:18 (NIV)

The Resurrection of the Dead — 1 Corinthians 15:12-26

After this I looked, and there before me was a great multitude that no one could count, from every nation, tribe, people and language, standing before the throne and before the Lamb. They were wearing white robes and were holding palm branches in their hands.
Revelation 7:9 (NIV)

The Bible Does Not Support the Teaching of Reincarnation

And as it is appointed for men to die once, but after this the judgment.
Hebrews 9:27 (KJV)

Chapter Three
Overshadowed by God's Faithfulness — Rose's Testimony

I am Rose, the third and youngest child born into an Italian Catholic family. I was a happy child with many warm memories of family, trips, and holidays until age ten when a stranger entered my school building and molested me. The police came to the school and took me to the hospital. My thoughts were that I might have done something wrong or something bad. I felt shame.

I made visits to the police station to view line-ups of men who I might recognize. These visits also included viewing pictures of possible suspects. I was told not to tell anyone about what happened. This was how these situations were handled in those days. I remember not being so happy anymore and becoming fearful with many nightmares. Sickness became part of my childhood. I had anemia, scarlet fever, allergies, and bronchial problems. Later, I was diagnosed with asthma.

My older siblings were married during my pre-teen years, leaving me as the only child at home. My mother, who had emotional problems, gradually grew worse and was diagnosed with schizophrenia. My dad did not know how to handle her blow-ups and anger. He retreated to the corner bar more frequently to avoid dealing with her.

In looking back, I see that I always needed to have a boyfriend. I ended up quitting school to get married the day after I turned seventeen with my parent's approval. I wanted my own family and dreamed of "living happily ever after." Drinking became a part of my life early in our marriage, and it turned into an addiction. My husband had his own gambling addiction. Life was not turning out as I had wanted. I did not get pregnant, and I worked many years even though a career was not my goal.

I Am Blessed With Children

After several years of marriage, we adopted an adorable little three-year-old girl. Eight months later, we adopted a charming three-week-old baby boy. Now, my family's dream was finally coming true. Five years later, I became pregnant and gave birth to a delightful baby boy. It felt as if our family was now complete. But instead of a life of "happily ever after," our addictions worsened, and I felt more guilty than ever before. I had prayed for a family, but now I was not taking them to church or teaching them about God. I was drinking and driving with my children in the car. Because I was making wrong decisions, shame surrounded me again. My health deteriorated. I had many severe asthma attacks despite weekly allergy shots, and I was hospitalized frequently for breathing treatments and oxygen.

My desire of "happy ever after" did not materialize. We had many good times, but we battled a lot over my husband's addiction that had caused some big issues in our marriage and family life. Drinking was my answer. This time in our lives was very discouraging and depressing.

Jesus Comes to Live In Me — Delivered From Alcoholism

At age 33, two friends shared with me about asking Jesus into my heart. I did, and He did! He came into my heart and took up residence. Miraculously, I was freed from alcoholism the day I accepted Christ. Now, for sure, we were going to be "fixed" and be a happy family. It did not work that way. We had many new difficulties since I was not drinking, and I started to attend church regularly. I was water baptized to some of my family's displeasure. They really didn't want to hear about the changes in my life that were so good for me. I was filled with the Holy Spirit with the evidence of speaking in tongues. No one wanted to hear about that either. I felt that my loved ones would want to have what I had, but most did not. Some friends and family accepted Christ. I felt that God had given me this Scripture promise:

They replied, "Believe in the Lord Jesus, and you will be saved — you and your household."
Acts 16:31 (NIV)

I expected it to happen quickly. It didn't!

My Marriage Dissolves

Twenty-four years after my wedding, the death of my marriage took place in the form of divorce. I was now 40 years old. We lost everything in the course of the divorce. We had bad credit. I went on welfare. My family did not believe in divorce, and they definitely didn't believe in being on welfare. No one in my family had ever been on welfare. I was ashamed again and feeling very guilty. I felt like I was a failure. In my eyes, my family abandoned me, and I became more discouraged. Fear of the future caused a lot of stress. I made some bad decisions. Anger and bitterness filled my heart. I went back to finish high school, and I graduated. I worked three part-time jobs to get off welfare. By this time, I was raising one child. I was able to trade a keyboard organ to get a car to drive to work. Other people helped me with food and gave me love offerings of cash.

I worked hard to get off welfare, but I had no medical insurance. I got sick again and had to be hospitalized with serious breathing issues, which caused me to go back on welfare. One of the times I was ill, I went into respiratory failure and almost died.

Tokens For Good from a Faithful God

There is a little phrase "token for good" in the King James Version in the Book of Psalms. [Dianne — Rose and I encouraged each other and spoke of this promise often. Through the years, we can testify the Lord Himself gave Rose and I tokens for good continually — little signs that He was near.]

> *Give me a sign of your goodness, that my enemies may*
> *see it and be put to shame, for you, Lord, have helped me*
> *and comforted me.*
> Psalm 86:17(NIV)

My life was a mess, and still, God gave me "tokens for good."

- Two of my children accepted Christ and His love. (I am praying for the third child.)
- Our needs were always met.
- Our phone was never shut off; neither were other utilities.
- The rent was always paid. With one child to raise, I eventually had to live with other families in my church.
- I started a home daycare, cleaned houses, and took care of elderly ladies to increase my finances.

At age 48, I finally got a full-time job with a company owned by Christians. That job, along with babysitting, changed my financial situation. My asthma attacks diminished, and there were fewer hospital stays.

Because I Love You

God had given me another Scripture promise to stand on from Isaiah 43:4 (NKJV):

> *Since you were precious in My sight, you have been*
> *honored, and I have love you; Therefore I will give men*
> *for you, and people for your life.*

This is a list of some of the ways this Bible verse was fulfilled in my life:

- One of the business owners (where I was employed) financed a trip for me to visit my oldest son, who had graduated from a university in Europe. I traveled to England!

- I was then given a trip to visit a ministry in Africa and be a part of their English-speaking school. I ministered to children in orphanages and a hospital.
- I went to Honduras to stay with missionary friends and again had the opportunity to minister the Word of God and be a part of their worship services.
- I was able to be at my daughter's graduation from a Bible school in Florida.
- I was given extra dividend pay just in time to help my son have a beautiful wedding celebration as he married his childhood sweetheart.
- I was able to minister to my precious sister and my mom as they approached death. God was restoring my family relationships.
- My brother gave me gas money to attend family functions.
- My wages increased so much I worked only one full-time job!

Good things happened! We have to see that God is always working in our lives, and it may take more time than we think. Along with the good things I have already listed, during these same years, God changed my heart from the inside out, one circumstance at a time:

- I had to become truthful and obedient.
- I had to face my unforgiveness toward many people in my life. Unforgiveness is not a word found in the dictionary. In the Christian world, the term "unforgiveness" means that a person is not forgiving a person in their heart.

They carry a burden until forgiveness is
given to another.
- I had to see my bitterness, my self-pity, and
my perfectionism.
- I had to recognize the disappointment and
guilt I was feeling with my decisions.
- I had to forgive myself.
- I had to stop judging some of my adult
children's decisions.
- I had to forgive my children.
- I had to acquire endurance with the right
attitude as I faced my strained relationships. I
was learning to persevere.
- I had to accept my part in the death of my
marriage and repent for my part.
- I had to acknowledge my hatred of
irresponsible men.

I learned how to talk to God as I faced being alone. I
reminded God that being alone was not in my "dreams of
life." I thought I would marry again and "live happily ever
after." I desired these changes and longed to be taken care of
financially.

Trials Come on Every Side

Instead of the security I longed for, my entire situation
made a turn for the worse. The company I was working for
closed its doors after fifteen years of steady employment for
me. My church of fifteen years had many problems, and I
needed to leave and find a healthy church. This was a difficult
decision for me, and I had to seek Christian counseling to
make the correct decision for my life.

Building Walls Between God and Me

I started pulling away from God, and that got my attention!
I was able to see I was building a wall between God and me. I
did not want to talk to Him about family or church or where I

would get my finances from? I didn't want to talk to God about it because this turn of events was very scary for me. I became fearful of the future. I felt so insecure in making decisions. I felt ashamed and broken!

The wall between God and me had names written on it: ANGER, BITTERNESS, FEAR for TODAY, FEAR of the FUTURE, RESENTMENT, SHAME, BROKENNESS, INSECURITY, FEAR of MAKING DECISIONS, SELF-HATRED.

God graciously led me by the Holy Spirit to a place where I would experience a freedom I had never known before. Bondages would go, chains would fall off! This is the ministry of Jesus and the Holy Spirit who was promised to us:

> *The Spirit of the Lord is on me, because he has anointed me to proclaim good news to the poor. He has sent me to proclaim freedom for the prisoners and recovery of sight for the blind, to set the oppressed free.*
> Luke 4:18 (NIV)

Deliverance From the Hand of My Faithful God

I entered a twenty-week program for Christians who had past or present addictions and struggled with relational idolatry.

- I had to allow God to heal the deep wounds of molestation.
- I had wounds from not being allowed to tell anyone.
- I needed healing from the effects of my mom's emotional illness on my life. (breaking generational curses)
- God cleansed the effect that my dad's drinking had on me, and my dad's choice to ignore helping with my mom's illness. (irresponsibility)

- There were more layers of unforgiveness from which I had to be set free in my inner being.
- My "victim" mentality had to change along with more bitterness that emerged.

I was now looking for another job which caused fear and stress. I had to deal with keeping everything bottled inside. I hated myself and had to confess many old, incorrect mindsets. This entire season was very humbling. The process was humbling and brought many tears. I had to continue to be honest about myself and persevere.

Beloved, I pray that you may prosper in all things and be in health, just as your soul prospers.
3 John 1:2 (NKJV)

I was estranged from one of my sons for years, and God has restored our relationship. Most of my adult children's relationships are very good, and my six wonderful grandchildren dearly love me. At present, I have been attending a fine church for fourteen years, and peace dominates my heart. I am fulfilled in who I am — I am the daughter of the King of Kings.

After you have suffered for a little while, the God of all grace, who has called you to His eternal glory in Christ, will Himself restore you, secure you, strengthen you, and establish you.
1 Peter 5:10 (BSB)

God has done all this for me. He is creating new memories by helping me focus on Him and realize the excellent work He has done to bring me from where I was to who I am now. God reminded me what I spoke at my mother's funeral. As previously stated, my mom suffered from the mental illness of schizophrenia. She accepted Christ into her heart after my dad died. Her years after that were spent in a nursing home as she required twenty-four-hour care. In the last five years of her life, I attended to her personal needs. She had been an embarrassment to me for years because of her strange ways. Taking care of her was not an easy task for me. She had been separated from many family members by her inappropriate behavior. I told God I did not have the grace to deal with her conduct. I heard these words in my heart:

But He gives more grace. Therefore He says: "God resists the proud, but gives grace to the humble."
James 4:6 (NKJV)

Ouch!! He showed me that instead of trying to change my mother, I needed to change. Repentance was required, and I had to be obedient by adjusting and moving forward. That was accomplished with God's help, and I began to love my mom. I was able to pray with her and help her with the hurts that had caused her to be so angry with others—she forgave them. At age 94, mother suffered mini-strokes, deteriorating quickly. She told me one day that she loved me without me saying it first. This was a special treat to me as she was not one to express herself freely at all in the past. She also told me three times that she loved Jesus, and I knew she was ready to meet Him. A part of what God gave me to speak at her funeral was this verse:

A good reputation is more valuable than the most expensive perfume. The day one dies is better than the day he is born!
Ecclesiastes 7:1 (TLB)

My mom's life as a young girl and in later years were difficult years filled with hurts, financial hardships, and broken relationships. Her family may have thought that success and achievement were the most important things in life. My mom may not have measured up to their standards. In the end, my mom forgave and loved her family. Her family forgave and loved her, and all was reconciled.

Jesus taught the people:

And He said to them, "Take heed and beware of covetousness, for one's life does not consist in the abundance of the things he possesses."
Luke 12:15 (NKJV)

Most important of all, Mom loved Jesus! My mom's life and my life were made beautiful with time. In life, we make mistakes that affect our families and others around us. Others can cause struggles which include suffering.

He has made everything beautiful in its time. He has also set eternity in the human heart; yet no one can fathom what God has done from beginning to end.
Ecclesiastes 3:11 (NIV)

If we cooperate with God, He can create a depth in our character that is extraordinary. Our struggles can refine us or define us. We get to choose. Suffering can make us better or worse. We get to choose.

Zero Hospital Occurrences!

Today, I can embrace contentment even though I have remained single for thirty-five years. I am currently enjoying financial stability. I have owned my own home for sixteen years. I have been employed as a bookkeeper at a company for twelve years. I am semi-retired, working only two days a week. My health is much better than it was in my younger days. I have had zero hospital occurrences. I have found God to be Faithful and True. You can trust Him, too!

Summary

Rose's story spotlights how to walk with God day in and day out. Her life illustrates how God is with us, and He is always working for good in our lives, but…His work takes time. We have to persevere and endure. God did not give Rose (or us) a spirit of fear. Fear is the opposite of faith. Rose conquered her fears as her faith grew by worship, attending church, reading the Word of God, praying to God, receiving godly counseling, and believing in God's faithful character. She stood on the promises of God. Rose came to believe a true promise she could trust:

The Lord will rescue me from every evil attack and will bring me safely to his heavenly kingdom. To him be glory for ever and ever. Amen.
2 Timothy 4:18 (NIV)

Overshadowed by God's Faithfulness — Rose's Testimony

ACTS Prayer

Worship God as Faithful and True. Write out your prayers in the spaces.

Adoration: I praise you Father God because you are faithful and true, and I can trust you in all the affairs of my life.

Confession: Lord, I have allowed anxiety and worry to undermine my complete trust in you.

Lord, my bitterness and resentment have made my heart hardened. Forgive me. Lord, I resist change and find myself disobeying you. Help me to be faithful to You.

Thanksgiving: Thank you, Lord, for delivering me from anger, bitterness, resentment. Thank you for all You have done for my family and me.

Supplication: Thank you, Lord, for sending me good counselors. I pray for people to get guidance and counseling. I pray for you to open your Word to those who are seeking your face, and for those who are in angry and bitter like I was.

Overshadowed by God's Faithfulness — Rose's Testimony

Process What You Have Learned

1. Did you grow up reading the Bible? Were you raised in a certain denomination?

2. Could you relate to Rose's story when she said that people witnessed to her? Have you had that experience? Who witnessed to you?

3. What are your expectations in life? Do you want "happily ever after"?

4. Have you had financial problems like Rose?

5. Rose was angry because people didn't take responsibility. Are you angry at other people? Why?

Overshadowed by God's Faithfulness — Rose's Testimony

The Biblical Worldview on Deliverance

Biblical References

Impure Spirits or Unclean Spirits — Mark 1:27; Luke 4:36; Acts 5:16; Luke 6:17-19; Matthew 12:43-45

Whenever the impure spirits saw him, they fell down before him and cried out, "You are the Son of God."
Mark 3:11 (NIV)

Jesus Gives Authority to Men — John 14:12; Mark 6:7; Acts 5:16; Acts 8:7; Mark 16:15-18

Jesus called his twelve disciples to him and gave them authority to drive out impure spirits and to heal every disease and sickness.
Matthew 10:1 (NIV)

False Prophets — Ezekiel 13:9; Matthew 7:15-20; 1 John 4:1-3

A false prophet will deny that Jesus came in the flesh and lived on the earth. A false prophet will teach there is no heaven or hell.

But there were also false prophets among the people, just as there will be false teachers among you. They will secretly introduce destructive heresies, even denying the sovereign Lord who bought them — bringing swift destruction on themselves.
2 Peter 2:1 (NIV)

Heaven and Hell Are Real Places — Matthew 25:41-46

◆ Hell is mentioned thirty-five times in the NKJV.

◆ Heaven is mentioned six hundred ninety-two times in the NIV New Testament.

We are living in a culture that has changed over several decades. Concepts such as heaven and hell used to be common knowledge and part of the belief system for Americans. Many people do not believe any longer that these are real destinations. The fact that they don't believe doesn't change the reality that heaven and hell exist.

Jesus told us these things when He was on the earth. Jesus taught about heaven and hell. He wanted the people to have the truth. What happens if people don't believe in the Bible? They die in their sins. Turning to Jesus, repenting of sin takes away their sins.

When we give our lives to Jesus, we need to find out what the Bible says. The Bible contains the truth that we can live by every day. Hell is a real place. Jesus rescues us from hell on earth and hell in eternity.

When I came to comprehend that God is always with me, it was such a comfort to my soul. Think about it...you are not alone in this chaotic, crazy world in which you live, and...this is not your home.

Satan Is Real — Matthew 4:1-11; James 4:7

> *Surely He shall deliver you from the snare of the fowler*
> *and from the perilous pestilence.*
> Psalm 91:3 (NKJV)

The fowler is an interesting type. He's a person who sets snares to catch birds. He's a hunter of birds. The fowler is a type of Satan. Do you resist the devil? Are you aware of his lies? Do we really have to be concerned about the devil?

> *Be sober, be vigilant; because your adversary the devil*
> *walks about like a roaring lion, seeking whom he may*
> *devour. Resist him, steadfast in the faith, knowing that*
> *the same sufferings are experienced by your brotherhood*
> *in the world.*
> 1 Peter 5:8-9 (NKJV)

Jesus shows us how to fight the devil in Matthew 4:1-11. Several times Jesus says: "It is written." We have to know what the Word says!

There is a verse in the Book of Isaiah 14:12-15 that describes Satan's story — the fallen angel. He wants worship. We worship only the Most High God and Jesus Christ, the only begotten Son of God.

Chapter Four

Overshadowed by Angels I — Zechariah's Testimony

The First Angelic Visitation of Luke's Gospel

Angels! Angels! Angels! The year is around 6 BC. There hasn't been any prophetic voice heard in 400 years, and suddenly angels appear declaring wonderful promises … hope streams on light beams to earth! The time of promise has come! In the Gospel of Luke, we read a series of fascinating stories where people are seeing and talking with angels.

For years I breezed over Luke 1:1-4 and went right to one of my favorite stories about Zechariah and Elizabeth. Let's look at these verses together before we move on to their story.

> *Many have undertaken to draw up an account of the things that have been fulfilled among us, just as they were handed down to us by those who from the first were eyewitnesses and servants of the word. With this in mind, since I myself have carefully investigated everything from the beginning, I too decided to write an orderly account for you, most excellent Theophilus, so that you may know the certainty of the things you have been taught.*
> Luke 1:1-4 (NIV)

In the Gospel of Luke, we find many special features.[1] This is the most comprehensive of the four Gospels. The general vocabulary and diction show that the author was educated. He makes frequent references to illnesses and diagnoses. Luke stresses Jesus' relationships with people, emphasizes prayer, miracles, and angels; records inspired hymns of praise; gives a prominent place to women. Most of what we read in Luke 9:51-18:35 is not found in any other Gospel.[2]

"Many people have set out to write accounts." There was a lot of interest in Jesus, and many people had material for an accurate and complete account of Jesus' life, teachings, and ministry. Because the truth was important to Luke, he relied heavily on eyewitness accounts.[3]

- Messianic Prophecies were fulfilled among the disciples. "Eyewitness reports" — Everything said and done by Jesus was public and accredited by thousands of witnesses. This brings us back to our definition of a "testimony" from the Introduction. We want to make certain a testimony is true.
- As a medical doctor, Luke knew the importance of being thorough. He used his skills in observation and analysis to thoroughly investigate the stories about Jesus. His diagnosis: The Good News of Jesus Christ is true![4]

Theophilus means "one who loves God." The Book of Acts, also written by Luke, is likewise addressed to Theophilus. This preface may be a general dedication to all Christian readers. Theophilus may have been Luke's patron, who helped to finance the book's writing. More likely, Theophilus was a Roman acquaintance of Luke's with a strong interest in the new Christian religion.[5]

Having a firm foundation that Luke's writings are true because he wrote "a careful account," let's go on to Luke 1:5, where we are introduced to Zechariah and Elizabeth, a priest and his wife. We read this description of them:

*Both of them were upright in the sight of God, observing
all the Lord's commandments and regulations
blamelessly.*
Luke 1:6 (NIV)

This verse has caused questions within me for years. How do we achieve this "living blamelessly?" We need to understand that these commendations of "observing all the commandments and regulations blamelessly" refer to legal righteousness. Zechariah and Elizabeth kept the Law of Moses. This was their reputation. Jesus was coming on the scene to bring a New Covenant based on Jesus' righteousness. This was the atonement for sin that He paid for on the cross. We, as Christians, live in the righteousness that Jesus purchased for us. This is different than keeping rules and regulations. Because of the cross and Jesus' blood that was shed, Jesus presents us "blameless" to His Father. We do not live in our own righteousness, but we live in the right standing that Jesus purchased for us.

Reading a few more verses and looking closer reveals a picture of Zechariah performing his priestly duties in the temple when something out of the ordinary occurs. He was about to experience the supernatural realm, and it would take him completely by surprise.[6]

> *Then an angel of the Lord appeared to him, standing at the right side of the altar of incense. When Zechariah saw him, he was startled and was gripped with fear. But the angel said to him: "Do not be afraid, Zechariah; your prayer has been heard. Your wife Elizabeth will bear you a son, and you are to give him the name John. He will be a joy and delight to you, and many will rejoice because of his birth, for he will be great in the sight of the Lord. He is never to take wine or other fermented drink, and he will be filled with the Holy Spirit even from birth."*
> Luke 1:11-15 (NIV)

Zechariah was "startled by the angel and gripped with fear!" Yes, I would be startled and fearful, too. Then the angel spoke and gave Zechariah information about the future. He informs him there will be a baby boy and tells him what to name his son! He describes who this little baby boy will become and tells how joyful Zechariah will feel. The angel foretells what God foresees "he will be great," and the baby isn't even conceived yet! The angel continues to explain the purpose ordained by the Lord for this one named John:

"Many of the people of Israel will he bring back to the Lord their God. And he will go on before the Lord, in the spirit and power of Elijah, to turn the hearts of the fathers to their children and the disobedient to the wisdom of the righteous – to make ready a people prepared for the Lord."
Luke 1:16-17 (NIV)

Who is this baby? The angel discloses the destiny of John the Baptist! The man who will "prepare the way for the Messiah." As for this miracle baby who isn't conceived yet, how can we understand the miracle? We find answers in the Book of Psalms. The forming of a human life in the womb is God's creating hand. This passage describes how precise and gentle God is when He creates us:

For you created my inmost being; you knit me together in my mother's womb. I praise You because I am fearfully and wonderfully made; your works are wonderful, I know that full well. My frame was not hidden from you when I was made in the secret place. When I was woven together in the depths of the earth, your eyes saw my unformed body. All the days ordained for me were written in your book before one of them came to be.
Psalm 139:13-16 (NIV)

You are fearfully and wonderfully made. That's how God sees you!

God was overshadowing Zechariah! He was an ordinary man who had an Almighty God overshadowing him. Zechariah's name means "Jehovah remembers." He is a praying priest. He and his wife Elizabeth had been praying for a child, but in her old age, Elizabeth was still barren. In the culture of that day, to be barren was considered a curse and a reproach. When they least expect it in their old age, an angel appears and tells the priest that he and his wife will have a baby!

Zechariah responds to the angel with doubt:

> *"How can I be sure of this? I am an old man and my wife*
> *is well along in years."*
> Luke 1:18 (NIV)

Do you see how Zechariah is acting so ordinary? Given the circumstances, would you have believed the angel's words? When Zechariah does not believe the angel's words, another unexpected event happens. We see the angel exert his power and authority.

> *The angel answered, "I am Gabriel. I stand in the*
> *presence of God, and I have been sent to speak to you and*
> *to tell you this good news. And now you will be silent*
> *and not able to speak until the day this happens, because*
> *you did not believe my words, which will come true at*
> *their proper time."*
> Luke 1:19-20 (NIV)

Unbelief. This story teaches us to keep believing the Lord even when our prayers have not been answered the way we think they should be. God always has a plan—it's a higher plan than our plan. We want to be people who carry belief in our hearts. The angel speaks with authority and tells Zechariah that he will not speak because of his unbelief!

The narrative moves from inside the temple where the supernatural is happening to outside the temple where the people are waiting. Where's Zechariah? The people wonder. The events unfolding this day at the temple were unusual, and the atmosphere was charged with the supernatural realm!

> *Meanwhile, the people were waiting for Zechariah and*
> *wondering why he stayed so long in the temple. When he*
> *came out, he could not speak to them. They realized he*
> *had seen a vision in the temple, for he kept making signs*
> *to them but remained unable to speak. When his time of*
> *service was completed, he returned home. After this his*
> *wife Elizabeth became pregnant and for five months*
> *remained in seclusion. "The Lord has done this for me,"*

she said. "In these days he has shown his favor and taken
away my disgrace among the people."
Luke 1:21-25 (NIV)

Can we imagine this scene together? The Bible tells us
Zechariah returned home "when his time of service in the
temple was ended." I imagine the people who were outside
the temple, who saw Zechariah when he couldn't speak,
excitedly ran to tell Elizabeth what took place. But they didn't
know the entire story. A few days would have passed before
Zechariah went home to Elizabeth. Would he tell her right
away? How would he communicate such news to her? She
might have begun the conversation asking with excitement: "I
was told that strange things occurred during your time at the
temple. What happened that you lost your voice?" Zechariah
would have written her a note. The note might have said:
"You are going to have a baby boy, Elizabeth. An angel told
me so!" Elizabeth would be delighted with the news. She
believed right away and knew that God had overshadowed
her with His favor. Her "disgrace" of barrenness would be
gone. Children were regarded as blessings from God. She was
saying "Yes" to this pregnancy and "Yes" to God. Do you
suppose that she and her husband had long ago ceased
praying for a child when Elizabeth was past the childbearing
years?

This miracle in Elizabeth's body parallels the miracle of
Abraham and Sarah. Sarah's womb was opened miraculously
to bring forth Isaac when she was past the childbearing years.
We see an Old Testament reference and a New Testament
reference with the exact miracle: from barrenness to childbirth!
Nothing is impossible with God. This story shows us the
sovereignty of God. We ask God in prayer—God answers in
His time. He knows how to answer our prayers, and we can
trust Him…well, we learn to trust Him, don't we? Zechariah
learned. Elizabeth learned. We learn to trust God in our
circumstances.

The Ministry and Characteristics of Angels

We do not see a cute little baby angel with wings in this story, do we? On the contrary, we envision a strong warrior angel standing in the temple who speaks with authority. His very presence instilled instant fear in Zechariah.

We are told about angels in the Word of God — angels are mentioned ninety-seven times in the New International Version of the Bible. Their ministry is to us as believers in Jesus Christ. We are heirs of salvation!

Are not all angels ministering spirits sent to serve those
who will inherit salvation?
Hebrews 1:14 (NIV)

Ministry of Angels

Angels are messengers sent by God, dispatched by Him with messages for mankind.[7]

- Angels reveal unknown truth — we can see this with Zechariah, and Mary, the mother of Jesus, with Daniel, with Joseph, who was betrothed to Mary.
- Angels give personal guidance — we see this is in the story of Joseph. Matthew 1:20, Luke 2:8-12 (NIV)
- Angels protect us and deliver us from enemies. Matthew 2:13 (NIV), the angel tells Joseph that Herod wants to kill Jesus.
- Angels protect and deliver us. Psalm 91:11-12 (NIV)
- Angels are spiritual beings. They have intellect, emotion, and free will. Matthew 28:5; 1 Pet. 1:12; Luke 2:13; 15:20 (NIV)
- Angels can be in only one place at a time. Daniel 9:21-23; 10:10-14 (NIV)
- They appear in the form of men. They are seen by some and not by others. Genesis 15:1-8; 2 Kings 6:15:17; Matthew 1:20 (NIV)

Back to our Zechariah story in Luke 1:57. We see another glimpse of Zechariah nine months later after John is born.

When it was time for Elizabeth to have her baby, she gave birth to a son. Her neighbors and relatives heard that the Lord had shown her great mercy, and they shared her joy. On the eighth day they came to circumcise the child, and they were going to name him after his father Zechariah, but his mother spoke up and said, "No! He is to be called John." They said to her, "There is no one among your relatives who has that name." Then they made signs to his father, to find out what he would like to name the child. He asked for a

*writing tablet, and to everyone's astonishment he wrote,
"His name is John." Immediately his mouth was opened
and his tongue set free, and he began to speak, praising
God.*
Luke 1:57-61(NIV)

See why I love this story! Zechariah hasn't spoken for nine months and eight days (give or take a few days). As soon as he writes, "the baby's name is John," Zechariah instantly speaks again! The Lord God gives him a prophecy and a song. God restores Zechariah's faith, removes unbelief, and fills him with the Holy Spirit. We serve a merciful God.

*All the neighbors were filled with awe, and throughout
the hill country of Judea people were talking about all
these things. Everyone who heard this wondered about it,
asking, "What then is this child going to be?" For the
Lord's hand was with him.*
Luke 1:65-66(NIV)

Good News! Good News! Good News!

These are the beginnings of the events that usher in the New Testament.

Overshadowed by Angels I — Zechariah's Testimony

ACTS Prayer

Worship God as your Creator. Write out your prayers in the spaces.

Adoration: Father, I worship you as my Creator and King. Jesus, I worship you because of who you are—God's Son. I worship you for creating me in my mother's womb. Lord, You deserve my worship, and I reverence You.

Confession: I realize what I did not know before that I am fearfully and wonderfully made by Your hand. You know me better than I know myself. I want to know You.

Thanksgiving: Thank you for the Cross, Jesus. I know that I am forgiven because you shed your blood for my sins on the Cross. Thank you for creating me and breathing life into me. Thank you that I am fearfully and wonderfully made. I thank you that forgiveness is a reality in my life. I forgive others because you have forgiven me.

Supplication: We pray for every woman and man that has been affected by abortion. We pray that they will recover. In the place of shame, Father, give them joy and peace. We pray for an end to abortion in America and all over the world.

Overshadowed by Angels I — Zechariah's Testimony

Process What You Have Learned

1. Have you read the story of Zechariah before?

   Were there details in the story that were new to you?

2. Have you or anyone you know gone through infertility issues? Share details.

3. Have you ever seen an angel? I know people who have seen an angel.

4. What new things have you learned about angels?

5. These stories are from the Gospel of Luke. Which Gospel is your favorite? Why?

Overshadowed by Angels I — Zechariah's Testimony

The Biblical Worldview on Abortion and The Hope We Have

Biblical References

Life Is Sacred — Romans 15:13

> *For You created my innermost parts; You wove me in my mother's womb. I will give thanks to You, because I am awesomely and wonderfully made; Wonderful are Your works, And my soul knows it very well. My frame was not hidden from You when I was made in secret, and skillfully formed in the depths of the earth; Your eyes have seen my formless substance; And in Your book were written all the days that were ordained for me, When as yet there was not one of them.*
> Ps.139:13-16 (NASB)

God Calls Abortion Sin — Sin Can Be Forgiven — Jeremiah 7:9; Psalm 106:37

> *Thou shalt not murder.*
> Exodus 20:13 (NKJV)

> *If we say that we have no sin, we are only fooling ourselves and refusing to accept the truth. But if we confess our sins to him, he can be depended on to forgive us and to cleanse us from every wrong. And it is perfectly proper for God to do this for us because Christ died to wash away our sins. If we claim we have not sinned, we are lying and calling God a liar, for he says we have sinned.*
> 1 John 1:8-10 (TLB)

Jesus Died For All Sin — You Can Be Forgiven — Luke 24:27; Ephesians 1:7; Acts 13:38; Matthew 26:28

> *Peter said to them, "Repent, and each of you be baptized in the name of Jesus Christ for the forgiveness of your sins; and you will receive the gift of the Holy Spirit.*
> Acts 2:38 (NASB)

God Does Not Condemn You — The Lord Removes Guilt and Shame

> *For God did not send his Son into the world to condemn the world, but that the world through Him might be saved.*
> John 3:17 (NKJV)

> *Who is he who condemns? It is Christ who died, and furthermore is also risen, who is even at the right hand of God, who also makes intercession for us.*
> Romans 8:34 (NKJV)

Forgive Yourself — Receive Hope and Love — Romans 8:24; Romans 15:4; Isaiah 61:1-2

> *Now hope does not disappoint, because the love of God has been poured out in our hearts by the Holy Spirit who was given to us.*
> Romans 5:5 (NKJV)

> *If our hearts condemn us, we know that God is greater than our hearts, and he knows everything.*
> 1John 3:20 (NIV)

Chapter Five
Overshadowed by Angels II — Mary's Story

The Second Angelic Visitation of Luke's Gospel

In contrast to the first angelic visitation where the angel appeared to an elderly priest in the temple, we read on to find the same angel, Gabriel, appearing and speaking with a young girl named Mary in her home. She is a virgin betrothed to a man named Joseph.

> *Now in the sixth month of Elizabeth's pregnancy, God sent the angel Gabriel to Nazareth, a town in Galilee, to a virgin pledged to be married to a man named Joseph, a descendant of David. The virgin's name was Mary. The angel went to her and said, "Greetings, you who are highly favored! The Lord is with you." Mary was greatly troubled at his words and wondered what kind of greeting this might be. But the angel said to her, "Do not be afraid, Mary; you have found favor with God. You will conceive and give birth to a son, and you are to call him Jesus. He will be great and will be called the Son of the Most High. The Lord God will give him the throne of his father David, and he will reign over Jacob's descendants forever; his kingdom will never end."*
> Luke 1:26-33 (NIV)

> *How will this be," Mary asked the angel, "since I am a virgin?"*
> Luke 1:34 (NIV)

> *The angel answered, "The Holy Spirit will come on you, and the power of the Most High will overshadow you. So the holy one to be born will be called the Son of God. Even Elizabeth your relative is going to have a child in her old age, and she who was said to be barren is in her sixth month. For nothing is impossible with God."*
> Luke 1:35-37 (NIV)

As we learned in the last chapter, angels are God's messengers. The angel Gabriel gives Mary a message about her future just as he did to Zechariah. The first thing the angel tells Mary is that she is "highly favored." Mary was given special honor — she was made acceptable by the Most High. That is what "favor" is…we don't earn it…it is given freely. Favor.

Mary is also told not to be afraid. As humans living in a temporal realm, we respond with fear when we encounter the supernatural realm. The angel brings news of Mary's destiny — she was going to become the mother of the Son of God! She was instructed to name her baby Jesus. She asked a question seeking information: "How will this be?" Her question did not show any unbelief. The power of the Most High would overshadow Mary! Mary responds to the angel's words:

> *"I am the Lord's servant." Mary answered. "May it be to me as you have said." Then the angel left her.*
> Luke 1:38 (NIV)

I refer to Mary's response as her "Yes to God." Her answer meant total acceptance of the will of God for her life. Mary would carry in her womb "The Promise" God had given to the whole world. When God promises, He fulfills. Prophecies of the Messiah were well known to the Jews. For centuries Jewish women pondered the thought of carrying "The Messiah" in their wombs. They considered it a privilege. All of Israel was waiting for the Messiah. Every Passover celebration since the time of Moses pointed to the coming of the Messiah.

Mary is an example for our lives even though she lived two thousand years ago. Is it possible for us to have our "Yes to God" ready at all times like Mary? We can be in this group of faithful people who God can call on to fulfill His great plan. Mary was an ordinary young woman. Look deep down in your heart — do you believe God could overshadow you? Let's consider this truth: we are made worthy to participate with

God because of what God has done. We are not made worthy by what we have done. God promised to send the Messiah. In God's timing, Jesus came and fulfilled that promise. He taught men about the Father. He died to redeem us from our sins. When God loved the world and gave His only Son, we become favored by God the moment we believe in Jesus Christ. We become overshadowed by the power of the Most High. Thank you, Jesus, for your great love and for dying for us.

Mary Visits Elizabeth

Who is going to believe Mary's story about seeing and talking to an angel? Who is going to believe Mary is carrying a baby who is of the Holy Spirit? Will Joseph believe her? Who can Mary turn to? Mary remembers that the angel told her news of Elizabeth having a baby in her old age.

I love what happens here. Mary decides to journey to see Elizabeth. "Yes!" She says to herself. "Elizabeth will listen to my story about the angel. She will believe that this baby I am carrying is from the Holy Spirit." She hurries quickly to the house of Zachariah. Mary wasn't expecting the greeting she received.

At that time Mary got ready and hurried to a town in the hill country of Judea, where she entered Zechariah's home and greeted Elizabeth. When Elizabeth heard Mary's greeting, the baby leaped in her womb, and Elizabeth was filled with the Holy Spirit. In a loud voice she exclaimed: "Blessed are you among women, and blessed is the child you will bear! But why am I so favored, that the mother of my Lord should come to me? As soon as the sound of your greeting reached my ears, the baby in my womb leaped for joy. Blessed is she who has believed that the Lord would fulfill his promises to her!"
Luke 1:39-45 (NIV)

As Mary enters Elizabeth's house, the Bible tells us two events took place: the baby leaped in Elizabeth's womb, and

Elizabeth was filled with the Holy Spirit! Mary has not told Elizabeth any of her story yet. Not only did Elizabeth affirm Mary, but she experienced a glorious overshadowing of God's Presence within her own womb and within her own spirit. The presence of joy must have been radiating through the atmosphere of their home. This atmosphere of joy overflows into praise, thanksgiving, and worship of the Almighty God, and Mary receives a prophetic song from the Holy Spirit.

Mary's Song

And Mary said: "My soul glorifies the Lord and my spirit rejoices in God my Savior, for he has been mindful of the humble state of his servant. From now on all generations will call me blessed, for the Mighty One has done great things for me — holy is his name. His mercy extends to those who fear him, from generation to generation. He has performed   mighty deeds with his arm; he has scattered those who are proud in their inmost thoughts. He has brought down rulers from their thrones but has lifted up the humble. He has filled the hungry with good things but has sent the rich away empty. He has helped his servant Israel, remembering to be merciful to Abraham and his descendants forever, just as he promised our ancestors."
Luke 1:46-55 (NIV)

What a blessing for Mary to visit Elizabeth! A wonderful example is laid out for us to imagine a younger woman having a relationship with an older woman. We want to keep in mind that Elizabeth was well advanced in years, and she was experiencing a miracle in her body with an unexpected pregnancy. Can you envision the scene?

Isn't the Lord good to arrange for these two women to be together during their time of pregnancy? I can imagine them laughing and singing and chattering as they cook the daily meals, sew clothes for their babies, and prepare for childbirth. I like to think that Elizabeth shared every detail with Mary of the event in the temple when the angel appeared to Zachariah. Mary would be relieved, comforted by the news that both she and Zachariah met the Angel Gabriel! I wonder if this thought became one of Mary's favorite memories of her visit. Hearing of Zachariah's experience would have been a true confirmation in Mary's heart that the Messiah was about to step into the story of the world. Surely, Elizabeth and Mary shared their faith with each other.

These musings paint a lovely picture of the women who are mentioned in Titus 2.

> *Likewise, teach the older women to be reverent in the way they live, not to be slanderers or addicted to much wine, but to teach what is good. Then they can urge the younger women to love their husbands and children, to be self-controlled and pure, to be busy at home, to be kind, and to be subject to their husbands, so that no one will malign the word of God.*
> Titus 2:3-5 (NIV)

Was Mary with Elizabeth when her birth pains began? The Bible gives us one little line with no details. For three months, Mary and Elizabeth were affirming each other. Did Mary just leave when the birth of Elizabeth's baby was going to occur at any moment? The Bible doesn't tell us. We cannot add to the Scriptures, but we can imagine that Mary remained until the baby was born. I believe Mary's time with Elizabeth prepared her for the birth of Jesus. Mary was young, maybe even a teenager. When she left Elizabeth and Zechariah's home, Mary was facing six months of her pregnancy. Did she tell Joseph she was pregnant before she left to be with Elizabeth? If that was the case, Joseph had time to consider everything about their mysterious situation before she returned home from her visit. We will be looking at Joseph's story in the next chapter.

I am happy to consider this thought: Mary stayed for John's birth. Mary may have been there when Zechariah's speech was restored after his long silence. She would have heard him say with boldness: "His name is John," and she would have heard the gasp of amazement from all the people when he spoke! I find it delightful to consider Mary relived all these special moments on her journey home to see Joseph. I imagine she had a smile on her face all the way home.

As Mary traveled back to Nazareth, her mind must have been spinning as she processed the wonder of it all—messenger angels sent to earth and Messianic prophecies coming to pass! Glory! Glory! Glory! Elizabeth was giving birth to a prophet, and Mary was carrying the promised Messiah in her womb! Immanuel...God with us!

What Mary didn't know: Joseph saw an angel in a dream and the angel spoke to him!

Overshadowed by Angels II — Mary's Story

ACTS Prayer

Worship the God of power and might. Add your prayers in the spaces.

Adoration: Father, we adore and worship You as the God of all power and might. Your purpose will stand. I choose to please You and not men. You are Almighty and we dwell in the secret place of the Most High and under the Shadow of the Almighty where you protect us.

Confession: We worship you because you are the Lord our righteousness. I want you to determine my steps. When I go my own way, I stumble.

Thanksgiving: Thank you for your promise of abundance.

Supplication: Lord, we are grateful that your Word tells us you hear us. We know that we have to remain close to You. You draw us to You continually.

Overshadowed by Angels II — Mary's Story

Process What You Have Learned

1. Did you grow up knowing the Christmas Story?

2. What about Mary's story surprised you?

3. Have you ever thought what Mary did when she went to stay with Elizabeth?

4. Did you learn anything about angels in this chapter that was new to you?

5. Mary said her "yes to God" after she asked a few questions. What "yes to God" are you contemplating? When have you said "yes?" When have you said, "no?"

Overshadowed by Angels II — Mary's Story

Biblical Worldview of The Coming of Messiah

Messianic Prophecies

◆ Jesus is the Messiah. God promised to send a man like Moses into the world who would be: born of a virgin; from the line of King David; a prophet; the root of Jesse; He would be referred to as Immanuel (God with us), a Branch, Wonderful Counselor, Mighty God, Everlasting Father, Prince of Peace. He would come out of Bethlehem Ephrathah.

◆ Listed below are the Messianic prophecies that the Jews would have known.

◆ Jesus' sufferings were prophesied. He would have enemies…and be rejected.

◆ Messiah would be a King.

◆ Many details were prophesied about the Messiah.

Biblical References — Genesis 49:10; Deuteronomy 18:15-16; Psalm 69:21;Psalm 118:22; Psalm 110:1; Psalm 118:22; Psalm 132:11; Isaiah 7:14; Isaiah 11:1; Zechariah 9:9; Micah 5:2

"And I will put enmity between you and the woman, and between your offspring and hers; he will crush your head, and you will strike his heel."
Genesis 3:15 (NIV)

"I will bless those who bless you, and whoever curses you I will curse; and all peoples on earth will be blessed through you."
Genesis 12:3 (NIV)

The Lord said to me: "What they say is good. I will raise up for them a prophet like you from among their fellow Israelites, and I will put my words in his mouth. He will tell them everything I command him."
Deuteronomy 18:17-18 (NIV)

Just as there were many who were appalled at him – his appearance was so disfigured beyond that of any human being and his form marred beyond human likeness.
Isaiah 52:14 (NIV)

He grew up before him like a tender shoot, and like a root out of dry ground. He had no beauty or majesty to attract us to him, nothing in his appearance that we should desire him.
Isaiah 53:2 (NIV)

For to us a child is born, to us a son is given, and the government will be on his shoulders. And he will be called Wonderful Counselor, Mighty God, Everlasting Father, Prince of Peace. Of the greatness of his government and peace there will be no end. He will reign on David's throne and over his kingdom, establishing and upholding it with justice and righteousness from that time on and forever. The zeal of the Lord Almighty will accomplish this.
Isaiah 9:6-7 (NIV)

Chapter Six
Overshadowed by Angels III — Joseph's Story
The Third Angelic Visitation

We are introduced to Joseph in the Gospel of Matthew 1:18, and it is a very nondescript introduction.

> *Now the birth of Jesus Christ took place in this way.*
> *When his mother Mary had been betrothed to Joseph,*
> *before they came together she was found to be with child*
> *from the Holy Spirit.*
> Matthew 1:18 (ESV)

Because of this limited introduction, we are compelled to do a little digging. We know Joseph was a descendant of David, (Luke 1:17), but there must be more information. Let's look at the ancient biblical time when a woman was "pledged" or "betrothed" to marry a man. In the twenty-first century, our customs are very different than customs in the first century. To help our understanding of the story, we need to discover what were the marriage customs two thousand years ago.

There were two ceremonies in an ancient Jewish marriage: the betrothal (pledge) celebration and the wedding celebration with a space of time in between. A couple became engaged when their two families agreed to their union. When a public announcement was made, the couple became "betrothed" to one another. The father of the groom would pay a "purchase price" to the bride's father. The ceremony signified they were being set apart for each other, and their commitment at this time was considered binding and could be broken only by death or divorce. The couple did not come together intimately until after they were married in the second ceremony.

The groom would go to his father's house and prepare a room for them to live. The bride prepared for his return, but she did not know when he would come. Then, a shout went up, usually at night, with a surprise gathering and a torchlight procession with the groom and the groomsmen coming to get

75

the bride. The shout was made to forewarn the bride that the groom was coming. The groom was ready to take his bride home with him.

Because Mary and Joseph were pledged to one another, when Mary was found to be carrying a child (which must have meant Mary had been unfaithful to Joseph), this circumstance held a severe social stigma. According to Jewish civil law, Joseph had a right to divorce her, and the Jewish authorities could have her stoned to death.

> *Because Joseph her husband was faithful to the law, and yet did not want to expose her to public disgrace, he had in mind to divorce her quietly.*
> Matthew 1:19 (NIV)

When we are studying a particular scripture passage, it can be very beneficial to compare different versions of the Bible to help with understanding. This would be a good time to compare Matthew 1:19 from the New International Version to the Life Application Bible taken from The Living Bible.

> *Then Joseph, her fiancé, being a man of stern principle, decided to break the engagement but to do it quietly, as he didn't want to publicly disgrace her.*
> Matthew 1:19 (TLB)

This verse tells us Joseph was faithful to follow the law, and he was strict in keeping to it. Joseph had two choices: divorce Mary quietly or have her stoned. There was a third option that hadn't entered his mind. We find the third option in the next verse. God provides an option!

> *But as he considered these things, behold, an angel of the Lord appeared to him in a dream, saying, "Joseph, son of David, do not fear to take Mary as your wife, for that which is conceived in her is from the Holy Spirit. She will bear a son, and you shall call his name Jesus, for he will sav his people from their sins."*
> Matthew 1:20-21 (ESV)

Can you imagine Joseph's struggle? I can almost say for certain there was tossing and turning in Joseph's sleep at night. There had to have been a daytime consternation and bewilderment as he worked. Every thought would be consumed with perplexity: "How could Mary be unfaithful to me? What should I do? I don't want Mary to be stoned. I want to do the right thing. Did she really talk to an angel? I have my doubts. Who has ever heard of such a thing? Could her story be true? My best option is to divorce her quietly. I don't want to disgrace her in front of everyone. Yes, that is what I will do. I will divorce her quietly."

Our awesome God sent one of his angels to Joseph in a dream! God wanted Joseph to know there was a third option. God had a bigger plan. "Joseph, take Mary to be your wife." In my translation: "Joseph, marry Mary!"

The angel gives Joseph four points to ponder:

- Don't be afraid to take Mary home as your wife.
- The baby boy is from the Holy Spirit.
- Name him Jesus.
- He will save his people from their sins.

God wanted to give Joseph direction. The Bible continues to give us more understanding as we search the Scriptures. We find another Old Testament Messianic prophecy being fulfilled.

Therefore the Lord himself will give you a sign. Behold, the virgin shall conceive and bear a son, and shall call his name Immanuel.
Isaiah 7:14 (ESV)

All this happened in order to fulfill what the Lord had spoken through the prophet [Isaiah]
Matthew 1:22 (AMP)

God wants to give us direction. God provides wisdom for us. He wants us to ask for wisdom.

Count it all joy, my brothers, when you meet trials of
various kinds, for you know that the testing of your faith
produces steadfastness. And let steadfastness have its full
effect, that you may be perfect and complete, lacking in
nothing. If any of you lacks wisdom, let him ask God,
who gives generously to all without reproach, and it will
be given him.
James 1:2-5 (ESV)

I would like to tell you that God will send you an angel or give you a dream or a vision every time you need guidance. That wouldn't be true. I cannot promise you that. We have God's Word to give us guidance and wisdom. I pray you will have ears to hear what the Lord is saying to you as you face your particular circumstances. You can hear God's voice. Jesus promised that His sheep would hear His voice. Our decisions affect the lives of others. When we seek God's wisdom, we will make the best decisions. God keeps His promises, and He has promises for us as we apply His Word in this new era.

"For My thoughts are not your thoughts, nor are your
ways My ways," says the Lord. For as the heavens are
higher than the earth, so are My ways higher than your
ways, and My thoughts than your thoughts."
Isaiah 55:8-9 (NIV)

God wants to overshadow us with mercy, wisdom, favor, protection, and more. He uses people in our lives. Joseph was chosen to take care of Mary, which meant protecting her. We read on to discover how Joseph responded to the angel's message.

When Joseph woke up, he did what the angel of the Lord
had commanded him and took Mary home as his wife.
But he did not consummate their marriage until she gave
birth to a son. And he gave him the name Jesus.
Matthew1:24-25 (NIV)

Notice that Joseph obeys the angel immediately. He interpreted the dream as a command from God. All Joseph's doubts were quenched. We see Joseph's character emerging as the Scriptures unfold. He does not consummate the marriage until after Mary gives birth to Jesus. This is an important point. Joseph considered his role in this supernatural event to be a sacred trust from God. Jesus was conceived through a miracle of the Holy Spirit. The prophet Isaiah also promised a virgin-born child who would be called "Immanuel," a Hebrew term meaning "God with us." (Isaiah7:14) Isaiah's prediction was made 700 years before the birth of Christ.[8]

Why is this so important? In order for Jesus to qualify as the only One who could pay the price for our sins and restore our broken relationship with God, He must be fully human, totally sinless, and yet fully God.[10] Jesus was fully God because He was conceived by the Holy Spirit. Jesus had to be free from the sinful nature passed on to all other human beings from Adam. Because He was born of a woman, he was a human being. He was fully human and fully divine.

Joseph's story is unfolding for us. Joseph was the man God chose to be Jesus' earthly father. He accepted his father role and demonstrated his "Yes to God" when he took Mary home as his wife. Joseph was obedient and honorable.

The couple would be faced with more decisions as the government decreed that there would be a census, and Joseph and Mary would have to register in the town of Bethlehem.

> In those days Caesar Augustus issued a decree that a census should be taken of the entire Roman world. (This was the first census that took place while Quirinius was governor of Syria.) And everyone went to his own town to register. So Joseph also went up from the town of Nazareth in Galilee to Judea, to Bethlehem the town of David, because he belonged to the house and line of David. He went there to register with Mary, who was pledged to be married to him and was expecting a child. While they were there, the time came for the baby to be

*born, and she gave birth in a manger, because there was
no room for them in the inn.*
Luke 2:1-7 (NIV)

God destined Joseph to be with Mary as they traveled to
Bethlehem when she was in the third trimester of her
pregnancy. The journey was about ninety miles and would
have taken them about four to seven days. It must have been a
difficult journey, and it wasn't a journey that they would have
chosen for Mary. Joseph knew God was with him. Mary and
Joseph must have wondered together about all these strange
events happening to them in regard to this "promised" child.
This is the promise:

*But thou, O Bethlehem Ephratah, who are too little to be
among the clans of Judah, from you shall come forth for
me one who is to be ruler in Israel, whose coming forth is
from of old, from ancient days.*
Micah 5:2 (ESV)

This unexpected journey of Mary and Joseph would fulfill a
Messianic prophecy about the little town of Bethlehem. We are
surprised by how God fulfilled it. He's always working; it
seems that we are always surprised.

It is of interest to note that Jesse and his sons, which
included King David, were from Bethlehem. God, as one
should expect, is the very master of detail. The meaning of the
name Bethlehem, the birthplace of Jesus Christ, is the "House
of Bread." Jesus Christ is known to the saints as "the bread of
life."[10]

*Then Jesus declared, "I am the bread of life. Whoever
comes to me will never go hungry, and whoever believes
in me will never be thirsty."*
John 6:35 (NIV)

The Fourth Angelic Visitation — The Shepherds

*And there were shepherds living out in the fields nearby,
keeping watch over their flocks at night. An angel of the*

*Lord appeared to them, and the glory of the Lord shone
around them, and they were terrified. But the angel said
to them, "Do not be afraid. I bring you good news that
will cause great joy for all the people. Today in the town
of David a Savior has been born to you; he is the
Messiah, the Lord. This will be a sign to you: You will
find a baby wrapped in cloths and lying in a manger."*

*Suddenly a great company of the heavenly host appeared
with the angel, praising God and saying,*

*"Glory to God in the highest heaven, and on earth peace
to those on whom his favor rests."*

*When the angels had left them and gone into heaven, the
shepherds said to one another, "Let's go to Bethlehem
and see this thing that has happened, which the Lord has
told us about."*

*So they hurried off and found Mary and Joseph, and the
baby, who was lying in the manger. When they had seen
him, they spread the word concerning what had been told
them about this child, and all who heard it were amazed
at what the shepherds said to them. But Mary treasured
up all these things and pondered them in her heart. The
shepherds returned, glorifying and praising God for all
the things they had heard and seen, which were just as
they had been told.*
Luke 2:8-20 (NIV)

This is our marvelous Christmas Story! As we study the
angelic visitations here, there, and everywhere, the story takes
on a glorious form. We see Mary, an ordinary girl, and Joseph,
an ordinary man, living in the little village of Nazareth. We see
Jesus humbly born in a manger because the inn was full.
Doesn't Jesus deserve better? After all, He's a King. But the
story isn't over. Our King is coming again. Yet, in all the
humility of that little manger, God lights up the sky, sends his
angelic messengers to the shepherds, sends joy to proclaim the
marvelous event that the Messiah, the promised Savior, has

been born on planet earth. Life will never be the same! Earth will never be the same! The next part of our story tells about wise men who followed a star and journeyed to Jerusalem to find the King of the Jews. What? Did they follow a star to find a baby king? This is unusual, too.

> *After Jesus was born in Bethlehem of Judea, during the time of King Herod, Magi from the east came to Jerusalem and asked, "Where is the one who has been born king of the Jews? We saw his star when it rose and have come to worship him."*
> Matthew 2:1-2 (NIV)

The Fifth Angelic Visitation — Joseph and The Escape to Egypt

> *When they had gone, an angel of the Lord appeared to Joseph in a dream. "Get up," he said, "take the child and his mother and escape to Egypt. Stay there until I tell you, for Herod is going to search for the child to kill him."*
>
> *So he got up, took the child and his mother during the night and left for Egypt, where he stayed until the death of Herod. And so was fulfilled what the Lord had said through the prophet: "Out of Egypt I called my son."*
> Matthew 2:13-15 (NIV)

When we know about prophecy, it is interesting to see the prophecies fulfilled. This is another example of how Joseph fulfilled the prophecy in Hosea. He was being guided by God.

> *When Israel was a child, I loved him, and out of Egypt I called my son.*
> Hosea 11:1 (NIV)

It is exciting to read about the many prophecies that were fulfilled; promises for thousands of years were coming to pass. History records that Herod was so obsessed with the news that a king was being born he called for the wise men to be brought to him and asked them what time the star appeared.

He was afraid that this king would one day take his throne. He commanded the wise men to go and find this king and then come back and report their findings to him. Herod said he wanted to worship the new king. The Bible tells us what Herod's real intentions were for this new king — and they weren't good. There was evil in Herod's heart. The wise men did not go back to Herod because they were warned in a dream.

When Herod realized that these wise men ignored his command, he was furious, and he gave orders to kill all the boys in Bethlehem and its vicinity who were two years old and under, in accordance with the time he had learned from the wise men. This is one of the saddest verses in the Bible, and it is another prophecy coming to pass. What was said through the prophet Jeremiah 31:15 was fulfilled:

Thus says the Lord: "A voice is heard in Ramah, lamentation and bitter weeping. Rachel is weeping for her children; she refuses to be comforted for her children, because they are no more."
Jeremiah 31:15 (ESV)

The Sixth Angelic Visitation — The Return to Nazareth

After Herod died, an angel of the Lord appeared in a
dream to Joseph in Egypt and said, "Get up, take the
child and his mother and go to the land of Israel, for
those who were trying to take the child's life are dead."
Matthew 2:19-20 (NIV)

Even though there is not much written about Joseph's life in the Gospels, three angelic visitations took place specifically to guide Joseph. These are wonderful glimpses for us to see how God was there to help Joseph as he fulfilled his purpose as protector of Mary and Jesus. Joseph did not question the guidance and quickly obeyed the angel's instructions in every situation. We can be assured by Joseph's example when God has called us to fulfill our purpose on this earth; He will provide protection and guidance for us.

So he got up, took the child and his mother and went to
the land of Israel. But when he heard that Archelaus was
reigning in Judea in place of his father Herod, he was
afraid to go there. Having been warned in a dream, he
withdrew to the district of Galilee, and he went and lived
in a town called Nazareth. So was fulfilled what was said
through the prophets, that he would be called a
Nazarene.
Matthew 2:21-23 (NIV)

The Bible records that Joseph and Mary returned from Egypt and settled in the town of Nazareth. Both the Gospels of Matthew and Mark record that Joseph and Mary added to their family and had sons and daughters:

Isn't this the carpenter? Isn't this Mary's son and the
brother of James, Joseph, Judas and Simon? Aren't his
sisters here with us?" And they took offense at him.
Mark 6:3 (NIV)

Because the people of Nazareth saw Jesus grow up with them, a person who lived among them, they would not believe that Jesus was the Messiah. The Bible tells us that "they took offense at him."

We know that Joseph was a carpenter, and he would have trained Jesus in those skills. Jesus' ministry didn't begin until He was thirty years of age. Jesus lived an ordinary life in a town where all the people knew His family. Because of this, the people who knew Him wouldn't believe what Jesus told them about Himself.

> *"Isn't this the carpenter's son? Isn't his mother's name Mary, and aren't his brothers James, Joseph, Simon and Judas?"*
> Matthew 13:55 (NIV)

People don't want the Messiah to be a humble leader. What do they want? A person of great power and wealth? A great warrior? A magician? Jesus was born into humble circumstances on earth, and He is able to understand our struggles. He came to give us life — abundant life! He came to destroy the works of the devil. He came to die for our sins.

> *Who has believed our message and to whom has the arm of the Lord been revealed? He grew up before him like a tender shoot, and like a root out of dry ground. He had no beauty or majesty to attract us to him, nothing in his appearance that we should desire him. He was despised and rejected by mankind, a man of suffering, and familiar with pain. Like one from whom men hide their faces he was despised, and we held him in low esteem. Surely he took up our pain and bore our suffering, yet we considered him punished by God, stricken by him, and afflicted. But he was pierced for our transgressions, he was crushed for our iniquities; the punishment that brought us peace was on him, and by his wounds we are healed.*
> Isaiah 53:1-5 (NIV)

Joseph was faithful, wise, kind, obedient, and humble. By digging deeper into the Word of God, we have observed and been persuaded that Joseph was an honorable man who God overshadowed to fulfill his God-ordained destiny.

When we consider the Jewish wedding traditions in the story of Joseph and Mary, we come upon a beautiful revelation. We have been bought and paid for by our Savior. He has betrothed us to Himself. Jesus has gone to the house of His Father to prepare a place for us to live with Him forever. These are the words of Jesus:

> *My Father's house has many rooms; if that were not so, would I have told you that I am going there to prepare a place for you? And if I go and prepare a place for you, I will come back and take you to be with me that you also may be where I am.*
> John 14:2-3 (NIV)

Every believer is referred to as the Bride of Christ, and Jesus made a promise that He would come back for His Bride and take us with Him. We are waiting for that day and that place He has prepared for us to live with Him forever!

> *Let us rejoice and exult and give him the glory, for the marriage of the Lamb has come, and his Bride has made herself ready;*
> Revelation 19:7 (ESV)

The return of our Bridegroom Jesus Christ is closer than it has ever been! Are you ready for His return? Will He find faith in your heart?

Overshadowed by Angels III — Joseph's Story

ACTS Prayer

Worship God as your Protector. Write out your prayers in the spaces.

Adoration: Father, I worship you as my protector. You go before me, you are with me, and you will not fail me or forsake me. I will not fear or be overwhelmed.

Confession: I acknowledge my sin to you. I do not cover up my iniquity. You know all things. I confess, and I have great peace knowing that you forgive all my sin. Help me walk in your ways.

Thanksgiving: I thank you that I can take refuge in you. This refuge makes me sing for joy. You protect me. Thank you that those who love your name rejoice in You.

Supplication: I pray for all those who don't know you. Draw them under your wing and protect them. You are my hiding place. Protect me from trouble and surround me with songs of deliverance.

Overshadowed by Angels III — Joseph's Story

Process What You Have Learned

1. Joseph was a chosen man of God who was in the background and not in the spotlight. Is your life in the background or in the spotlight?

2. When it came to decisions, Joseph needed God's wisdom. Describe a time when God helped you make the right choice.

3. Did you know that there is another Joseph in the Book of Genesis who had dreams?

   Read about him in Genesis 37.

4. Did one thing stand out to you as we looked at Joseph's Testimony?

5. Have you stepped out in faith and said "Yes to God" in your life? By reading Joseph's story, do you know that God will guide you with every step you take when you call on Him?

Overshadowed by Angels III — Joseph's Story

Biblical Worldview of God's Protection

Biblical References

God Protects His People

*"Because he loves me," says the Lord, "I will rescue him;
I will protect him, for he acknowledges my name. He will
call on me, and I will answer him; I will be with him in
trouble, I will deliver him and honor him.*
Psalm 91:14-15 (NIV)

Jesus Prayed for Our Protection

*I will remain in the world no longer, but they are still in
the world, and I am coming to you. Holy Father, protect
them by the power of your name, the name you gave me,
so that they may be one as we are one.*
John 17:11 (NIV)

*While I was with them, I protected them and kept them
safe by that name you gave me. None has been lost except
the one doomed to destruction so that Scripture would be
fulfilled.*
John 17:12 (NIV)

*My prayer is not that you take them out of the world but
that you protect them from the evil one.*
John 17:15 (NIV)

God Gives Us Angels to Protect Us

*For he will command his angels concerning you to guard
you in all your ways; they will lift you up in their hands,
so that you will not strike your foot against a stone.*
Psalm 91:11-12 (NIV)

Jesus Is the Lamb of God

In a loud voice they were saying: "Worthy is the Lamb, who was slain, to receive power and wealth and wisdom and strength and honor and glory and praise!"
Revelation 5:12 (NIV)

For the Lamb at the center of the throne will be their shepherd; 'he will lead them to springs of living water.' 'And God will wipe away every tear from their eyes.'"
Revelation 7:17 (NIV)

They triumphed over him by the blood of the Lamb and by the word of their testimony; they did not love their lives so much as to shrink from death.
Revelation 12:11 (NIV)

Chapter Seven
Overshadowed by Light — Beth and Steve's Story

*I have come into the world as a light, so that no one who
believes in me should stay in darkness.*
John 12:46 (NIV)

There she lay, lingering in pain in a darkened spare
bedroom, on a couch, in her pajamas. Day and night were the
same — black. Day after day, night after night, the excruciating
pain tortured her. Was her destiny to slip slowly into the abyss
after suffering this constant tormenting pain in her head?
There was no hope in this place. There were no changes here
as days, weeks, and months dragged on. She felt unloved and
unwanted by God, but she believed in Him, wherever He was.
Her cries were directed to God as she begged for mercy. Did
He hear her moans? Did He see her despair? Did He care?

She screamed: "Why won't you love me? If you loved me, I
wouldn't be separated in this dark place from my husband
and my children, or my friends, or my nursing job, or my
church." She raged at God with her arm held high, and her fist
clenched: "You must hate me." She searched her heart. "What
have I done to deserve this never-ending torment?"
Hopelessness was the air she breathed. "I'm on a couch in
Cutlerville. Do you know where Cutlerville is?" She yelled at
the invisible God and sobbed to Him in her misery.

Her head hurt to look at light…any light. A tarp was put
up, so that not even a sliver of natural light could enter the
room. The only light came from the small digital clock placed
on the floor.

The diagnosis? A condition known as Intractable Migraine
Headache. Five years. She was in constant pain for five years,
pain that never completely subsided even after going to six
different physicians. Medications were prescribed. Even if a
medication did help, the effect lasted only for a short period of
time, and then the medicine lost its effectiveness. Doctors

91

would write another prescription. Endless medications seemed to be her destiny. The relentless cycle repeated itself: pain, doctors, medications, darkness; pain, doctors, medications, darkness…pain.

"Steve," Beth said to her husband in panic mode, "You have to take me to the emergency room. I can't bear the pain!" She was discharged from the hospital in just as much pain as when she arrived.

One doctor did a series of treatments in which he injected steroids and Botox into her scalp. She went for acupuncture treatments. She had an expensive food "toxicity" test and followed the recommended diet for several months. She was put on very expensive nutritional supplements for a period of time. Nothing worked. The cost was staggering.

She had tried her best to cope with the affliction on a daily basis, but as time passed, she had no other choice but to slowly drop out of life as the pain got progressively worse. She took a leave of absence from her nursing career. The cramped, dark room became her living space.

Out Of Rebound — Is This The Light?

Can you guess what pathway remained for her to take? She became a patient at the local pain clinic. Her doctor at the clinic said, "The medications you have been on since your condition began have put you into a state of what we call 'rebound.' This 'rebound state' actually makes the pain worse."

She was given other medications by IV for a period of time, so her nerve receptors could adjust to not having the original medications. Going through rebound treatment can be compared to going through withdrawal from addictive drugs. This meant she was unable to be alone. She lived with her in-laws for six weeks in their basement room. How gracious they were to their daughter-in-law. They drove her twice a day to a pain clinic. Twice a day.

Finally, the clinic doctor stated, "You are out of rebound."

She had a week of moderate pain, and then the high level of excruciating pain returned. She went back to the physician. After trying several additional drugs, the end diagnosis came.

"No one in Grand Rapids can help you," the doctor concluded.

Beth was referred to a nationally recognized neurological institute. The goal of the institute was to control her pain. It was a month-to-month process with little change as time passed. As the months dragged on, she became convinced that she was predestined to a dreaded existence of horrible pain, on a couch, in a dark room, living in her pajamas. The evidence was clear: she had already worn out several pairs of pajamas.

Now faith is the substance of things hoped for, the evidence of things not seen.
Hebrews 11:1 (NIV)

Beth was feeling like everything she loved and cared about had been snatched away from her. She loved her job as an RN, and that was yanked from her as well. It felt like everything was being stolen from her, and it looked to her like this dark life was going to be permanent. She lived a minimal existence. She only saw her husband and their three children when they came into her dark room. The children were in high school grades 9, 11, and 12. She was unable to function in their lives.

As a regular churchgoer, she hadn't attended church for more than a year. The only contact she had with society happened when church friends would come to visit her. She lived alone, waiting for God to take her home.

"Take me in my sleep," she prayed…every single night.

Beth Describes How God Manifested His Light

And God said, "Let there be light," and there was light.
Genesis 1:3 (NIV)

When I sit in darkness, the Lord will be a light to me.
Micah 7:8 (NIV)

Beth

At the end of March, five months after entering the black basement room, my dark gloom was pierced by a ringing telephone. Like a precision laser cutting a diamond, this simple telephone call became God's answer for me and there was light.

"Steve, you are going to think this is the craziest phone call you ever received!" said our friend from church.

"I am related to a woman who also has struggled with chronic migraines like your wife, and no medical treatment has helped her either. Our family found a pastor who has gifts of healing and the gift of discerning of spirits. He has been praying for her, and she is doing a lot better. The pastor is from out of state, and he is going to be in town for a couple of weeks. He has set aside time to pray with people.

"Are you interested in bringing your wife for prayer?" the friend asked.

Steve and I talked about this and decided that anyone who was a sincere Christian and wanted to pray for us would be welcome to do so.

Steve called the person hosting the meeting.

"Sure, we have room for you," he said. "If we have more than ten or fifteen people show up, we'll use our basement."

The Bible teaches us about these gifts:

> *Now, about the gifts of the Spirit, brothers and sisters, I do not want you to be uninformed. You know that when you were pagans, somehow or other you were influenced and led astray to mute idols. Therefore I want you to know that no one who is speaking by the Spirit of God says, "Jesus be cursed," and no one can say, "Jesus is*

94

Lord," except by the Holy Spirit. There are different
kinds of gifts, but the same Spirit distributes them. There
are different kinds of service, but the same Lord. There
are different kinds of working, but in all of them and in
everyone it is the same God at work. Now to each one the
manifestation of the Spirit is given for the common good.
To one there is given through the Spirit a message of
wisdom, to another a message of knowledge by means of
the same Spirit, to another faith by the same Spirit, to
another gifts of healing by that one Spirit, to another
miraculous powers, to another prophecy, to another
distinguishing between spirits, to another speaking in
different kinds of tongues, and to still another the
interpretation of tongues. All these are the work of one
and the same Spirit, and he distributes them to each one,
just as he determines.
1 Corinthians 12:1-11 (NIV)

So, one Sunday evening in mid-April, 2005, with me (Beth), in significant pain, Steve and I turned down this man's street and saw cars lined up on both sides. We arrived at the house to find the basement packed with people. After introductions, the pastor had a teaching time. The text was from the book of Daniel chapter 10:

A hand touched me and set me trembling on my hands
and knees. He said, "Daniel, you who are highly
esteemed, consider carefully the words I am about to
speak to you, and stand up, for I have now been sent to
you." And when he said this to me, I stood up trembling.
Then he continued, "Do not be afraid, Daniel. Since the
first day that you set your mind to gain understanding
and to humble yourself before your God, your words
were heard, and I have come in response to them. But the
prince of the Persian kingdom resisted me twenty-one
days. Then Michael, one of the chief princes, came to help
me, because I was detained there with the king of Persia.
Now I have come to explain to you what will happen to

95

*your people in the future, for the vision concerns a time
yet to come." While he was saying this to me, I bowed
with my face toward the ground and was speechless.*
Daniel 10:10-15 (NIV)

This text speaks of Daniel humbling himself and praying
for understanding. The angel speaking to Daniel told him that
his words were heard from the first day Daniel prayed. The
angel tells Daniel what circumstances existed to delay those
prayers. The pastor spoke of Nebuchadnezzar's dream of the
image with the head of gold, chest of silver, belly and thighs of
bronze, legs of iron, and feet of iron and clay. He pointed out
the spiritual forces of evil in each of these historical empires.
Another Scripture illustrates the point:

*For our struggle is not against flesh and blood, but
against the rulers, against the authorities, against the
powers of this dark world and against the spiritual forces
of evil in the heavenly realms.*
Ephesians 6:12 (NIV)

This particular spiritual force of evil Daniel spoke of had a
title: the Prince of Persia. As the pastor preached, questions
rushed into the minds of Beth and Steve: Was the power of
this dark world, and were the spiritual forces of evil in another
realm responsible for Beth's affliction? Had she been wrong to
think that all this was from God? She had been blaming Him
for so long!

Beth continued reflecting:

The Pastor then started the healing time with a short time of
teaching directly related to healing prayer: "We cannot
manipulate God. When we ask the Holy Spirit to be involved
in healing, something that normally takes six months may take
two. Something that normally may take a month takes a few
days or a week or two. If it happens tonight, it is a miracle."

When it was our time to go forward, he asked what I
wanted prayer for. We sat in two chairs in front of the pastor,

and I explained my situation. The pastor anointed me with oil and prayed for me. As soon as he touched me, my pain level shot up even higher, and I immediately held my head in my hands for a few moments.

After praying for me, the pastor asked Steve what he wanted prayer for.

Steve said, "The grace to deal with my situation."

Steve also said, "Due to surgery and radiation for kidney cancer that I had as a newborn, my pelvis is tilted, one leg is longer than the other, and I have a spinal curvature. But, at my age, there probably isn't anything that can be done about it."

Steve Is Healed!

The pastor looked directly at Steve and said, "The Holy Spirit can do a lot for you." He called everyone to gather around to watch. He anointed Steve with oil and said, "Put out your arms."

Steve put out his arms, holding his palms together. The pastor lightly touched the back of Steve's hands and commanded Steve's shoulders to line up in the name of Jesus Christ. Steve felt a little something but did not think too much of it.

Steve was seated in a chair. "Pick up your feet," the pastor said.

He took Steve's heels in the palms of his up-turned hands and said, "I push up a little; I don't pull. I am going to command your scar tissue to soften and your left hip to drop an inch in Christ's name."

As he commanded the spirit of asymmetry to come out of Steve's body, Steve's left foot started to move downward until both feet were even. Everyone who was gathered around could see it happen! As soon as Steve stood up, he felt as if he had an electric shock from above his knees to the bottom of his feet. He was also wobbling around with his arms out, trying to keep his balance when he started to walk.

Steve said, "Wow, this is really different!"

The pastor then had two more people seated in front of him. He smiled and said, "Sometimes it takes a while to sink in."

We left the house and, as we were walking across the front lawn, I wondered why I was in worse pain. Steve was trying to catch his balance.

On Monday of the following week, Steve stopped in our pastor's office.

He explained to him what had happened to him and said, "Help me understand this. If Christ is the only mediator between God and man, and we are not supposed to seek spiritists or mediums (1 Samuel 28:9), why did this take place as it did?"

The pastor replied, "You said that the visiting pastor did not claim to be able to manipulate God. This is different than what the Bible describes as the mediums and spiritists we are not supposed to have anything to do with."

The pastor then pointed out. "Would you have recognized this as coming from the hand of God if it just came slowly?"

Reflecting on this question, Steve realized if the experience had not been so dramatic, he would not have recognized this as the hand of God.

Back at home, I asked Steve, "Why aren't you wearing the lift in your shoe?" He had worn the lift for years.

"Because my feet are now even!" Steve picked up his feet to show me what had happened.

Steve received a miracle! I looked at his back and could tell the curve in his lower back was gone! I had not realized that a physical change had taken place. Over the years, five doctors told Steve that nothing could be done for his condition.

Because of this miracle in Steve's body, he was relearning to drive his stick shift car. His left foot was putting the clutch in faster than he was used to. He was also waking up in the night when his ankle bones would bang together in his sleep. Before his healing, his bones were not lined up, and he didn't have a problem at night. After a few days, his entire body adjusted to the changes.

In the middle of the week, the host of the healing service called Steve.

"How is your wife doing?"

"Well, actually not very well."

"At times, God grants these types of healings in stages to help us understand that we are to keep seeking Him," he explained. "How are you doing?"

"Seeing the changes in my legs was God's way of showing us that He still had His hand on our lives. I can really feel and see the changes, but my shoulders are still not square with the rest of my body."

"God is a God of completeness. I encourage you both to come back on Saturday."

Saturday came, and we arrived at the start of the healing time. The basement was packed once again. When it was our turn to go forward, I mentioned some things to the pastor that I had been wrestling with for nearly as long as I could remember, things that were in our family line.

"Now, we are getting to the bottom of it." The pastor exclaimed. "You are under the influence of a specific evil spirit which has been affecting your ancestors for three generations. This is what we refer to as a generational curse."

The Bible speaks of the sin of the fathers to the third and fourth generations. (Keep in mind this pastor's gift of discerning of spirits) This is what the Bible says:

> *"You shall not make for yourself an image in the form of anything in heaven above or on the earth beneath or in the waters below. You shall not bow down to them or worship them; for I, the Lord your God, am a jealous God, punishing the children for the sin of the parents to the third and fourth generation of those who hate me, but showing love to a thousand generations of those who love me and keep my commandments.*
>
> Exodus 20:4-6 (NIV)

Based on the type of spirit he described and the family history I could recall, I could see what he was saying was true. I now realize this spirit began to affect me early in my life. The pastor anointed me with oil. This time I did not experience the increase in pain when I was anointed. The pastor commanded this spiritual force to leave me in Jesus' Name. As the influence of the spiritual force left me, I felt as if a dam had suddenly broken inside of me. There was a time of weeping which I had no control over.

"Do you want prayer for anything, Steve?" asked the pastor.

"You have spent a lot of time with my wife, and there are many others waiting."

The host said, "Go ahead and ask."

"My shoulders still aren't aligned."

"Sit back in your chair again and stretch out your arms." He anointed Steve with oil and touched the back of Steve's hands as he had done the time before. We had been told that this pastor had the gift of the Holy Spirit to reveal what is happening as it happens. This time he commented as the Holy Spirit moved Steve's bones back and forth to bring them into alignment.

First, the left shoulder. "The left shoulder is moving forward; now it is moving back." He said all this in a tone that this movement was all that he expected. Steve could feel his shoulder blade continue to move.

"Now it's moving way back; now it's moving even further!"

When his shoulder blade was all the way back, Steve said that it felt as if someone had put a pipe wrench on his shoulder blade and twisted it. This was a distinct and powerful sensation but void of pain. Steve will never forget that sensation.

Before we left, the pastor spent some time advising us how to deal with our situations. He spoke of God seeing us as cleansed in Christ. We are to use the weapons of spiritual warfare (2 Corinthians 10: 3-5) to deal with the doubts and challenges the forces of evil throw at us. (Ephesians 6:12 fiery darts of the wicked) He spoke of how Satan is the master of lies and will seek to deceive us.

"Whenever the devil comes around to torment your wife, Steve, you have the authority to tell him to leave."

As we drove away in the car that evening, Steve thought, "Who am I to do that?"

The next weeks were a struggle as we continued to marvel at what happened to Steve, and yet, I wrestled with pain that ranged from moderate to severe at this point.

One day, Steve called the man who hosted the healing service. At the end of their conversation, the man mentioned he had just gotten home from the Healing Rooms.

Steve asked, "What are the Healing Rooms?"

He explained it was a nonprofit organization of volunteers who pray to help people deal with the same type of issues as the visiting pastor deals with. The volunteers practice authoritative prayer for healing and miracles by calling them forth in the name of the Lord Jesus Christ and for deliverance, that is, casting out evil spirits to set people free.

"Remember, Steve, healing is a process, while miracles are immediate," the man reminded.

The following Saturday, I was in severe pain. Steve loaded me up in the car and took me to the Healing Rooms. The lead volunteer who met with us gave us about forty-five minutes of personalized teaching time.

"Most Christians don't realize Christ has already accomplished our physical healing on the cross, just as He accomplished our salvation. As we seek spiritual healing in this life, we can also seek the manifestation of physical healing knowing we will have full healing in the next life."

He referenced the Bible text telling us to ask, seek, and knock in Luke 11:1-13.

He taught us to be careful how we word our prayers.

"Do not pray: 'God, you could heal me if you want to,' but pray 'God, I know you will heal me in your time.' We are to realize His time may be in the next life. When people have a long-term illness or condition, after a while, they can start to think God must not even love them because they know He has the power to heal but doesn't. Realizing God loves you despite your circumstances is important."

This is exactly what had been taking place in my mind. "God," I had cried, "You don't love me!"

The Healing Rooms volunteer gave me verses which speak of how much God loves me.

"Those verses don't apply to me," I said out loud. I was still convinced God did not love me.

"Satan lies to us so we will not believe the truth of God's Word. I am going to command a deaf and dumb spirit to leave you because you can hear and talk, but when you read these promises in the Bible, they are not being revealed to you in your spirit."

He anointed me with oil and commanded the deaf and dumb spirit to leave me in Jesus' Name. "You need to be bathed in prayer and reminded daily of the promises God gives us in His Word." He gave me a five-page handout with these scriptures on them and told me to read them out loud three times a day.

"The devil doesn't know what we think. When we read the Bible out loud and pray out loud, the devil is able to hear us and knows we are calling upon the name of Jesus."

The man who prayed then invited me, "Return to the Healing Rooms as many times as you need to."

After I had been to the Healing Rooms, in my darkness, I began to read aloud the Bible promises I had been given three times a day. Now, I had two sources of light: the clock and a flashlight. With the clock, I knew when to read my Scripture. With the flashlight, I illuminated God's Word. Over time, I began to see Jesus is the Light of the World.

The following week I read my Bible and said to Steve, "This applies to me!"

"Yeah, it does..." he said as if scratching his head and wondering why I couldn't see it before.

At this time, something else interesting happened. We were learning...

You, Lord, are my lamp; the Lord turns my darkness into light.
2 Samuel 22:29 (NIV)

He reveals the deep things of darkness and brings utter darkness into the light.
Job 12:22 (NIV)

Tell The Enemy "No!"

One of the teachings on the handout from the Healing Rooms was: We can be healed, and the devil will try to give us the same symptoms to make us think we have not been healed.

Honestly, this did not make sense to us. If a person has the symptoms, they have the problem, right?

We were to learn differently...firsthand!

Steve's scar tissue started to contract. Over several days a great tension developed between his rib cage and his pelvis, much like it was prior to his healing. One morning, he was asking himself, "Have I ever actually prayed for this specific condition?" He realized he hadn't. He started to pray, and before he said "Amen," the tension was gone.

Several months earlier, our pastor had offered to anoint me as described in James 5:13-16. It is called the Prayer of Faith:

Is anyone among you in trouble? Let them pray. Is anyone happy? Let them sing songs of praise. Is anyone among you sick? Let them call the elders of the church to pray over them and anoint them with oil in the name of the Lord. And the prayer offered in faith will make the sick person well; the Lord will raise them up. If they have sinned, they will be forgiven. Therefore confess your sins

103

*to each other and pray for each other so that you may be
healed. The prayer of a righteous person is powerful and
effective.*
James 5:13-16 (NIV)

Steve and I talked about this verse and decided that having
our pastor anoint me would be a good way to introduce some
of our church family to the Holy Spirit's power that we
experienced with Steve's healing.

The evening of my anointing, our children, an elder, and
two of the ladies of the congregation who had been praying
for me on a regular basis were present. Our pastor addressed
the small group. "Healing takes place in God's time. The text
in James says that the prayer of faith will heal, and it is not the
sick person having enough faith."

He anointed me, and everyone present prayed for me. I
thought about how my situation would not be an easy one for
any elder to deal with. How do you go about reassuring
someone that God cares for them in the midst of what appears
to be a hopeless situation? Yet, our elder had been faithfully
keeping in contact and visiting with me. When it was his turn
to pray, he wept with us. This is exactly what Jesus did with
Martha and Mary when Lazarus died. "Jesus wept."

I continued to struggle with my head pain. Steve and I
returned to the Healing Rooms.

Learning To Take Authority Through Jesus

The volunteer who met with us at our next Healing Rooms
visit explained. "After a spirit is cast out, it will try to return as
Jesus described in the Gospel of Matthew."

*"When an impure spirit comes out of a person, it goes
through arid places seeking rest and does not find it.
Then it says, 'I will return to the house I left.' When it
arrives, it finds the house unoccupied, swept clean and
put in order. Then it goes and takes with it seven other
spirits more wicked than itself, and they go in and live
there. And the final condition of that person is worse*

104

than the first. That is how it will be with this wicked generation."
Matthew 12:43-45 (NIV)

"You need to rebuke the devil when he comes to torment you," the volunteer explained.

"Who are we to rebuke the devil?" Steve said, stating again what he had thought at the end of the second prayer meeting in the basement.

The volunteer then taught us more about the spirit world that we contend with in spiritual warfare found in the Gospel of Matthew 4. The devil tempted Jesus in the wilderness. Jesus quoted Scripture, and He rebuked and conquered the devil. Jesus is THE WORD! Jesus gave us the authority to do this.

Then Jesus was led by the Spirit into the wilderness to be tempted by the devil. After fasting forty days and forty nights, he was hungry. The tempter came to him and said, "If you are the Son of God, tell these stones to become bread." Jesus answered, "It is written: 'Man shall not live on bread alone, but on every word that comes from the mouth of God.'" Then the devil took him to the holy city and had him stand on the highest point of the temple. "If you are the Son of God," he said, "throw yourself down. For it is written: "'He will command his angels concerning you, and they will lift you up in their hands, so that you will not strike your foot against a stone.'" Jesus answered him, "It is also written: 'Do not put the Lord your God to the test.'" Again, the devil took him to a very high mountain and showed him all the kingdoms of the world and their splendor. "All this I will give you," he said, "if you will bow down and worship me." Jesus said to him, "Away from me, Satan! For it is written: 'Worship the Lord your God, and serve him only.'" Then the devil left him, and angels came and attended him.
Matthew 4:1-11 (NIV)

The volunteer also pointed us to Luke 9 and 10 and showed us how the twelve apostles and seventy people were given the authority to cast out demons and went out and did so.

He also noted that apparently, they had not yet even been taught the proper way to pray because Jesus' teaching them the Lord's Prayer is recorded later in the Gospel of Luke.

"This type of authority is given to all believers," the Healing Room worker said. "Rebuking the devil must be done in the name of the Lord Jesus Christ whenever Satan comes around to steal, kill, or destroy our lives. This did not apply only to this situation, but any situation where there is a roadblock to having the proper relationship with Jesus."

After this visit, I truly began to believe the only way I would find relief from the pain was to rebuke Satan and completely humble myself and pray for the Holy Spirit to heal me. Steve and I began to rebuke Satan to break the pain. It was an intense time where we were directly facing our tormenter.

Steve said, "Satan, leave my wife alone. Flee from her in Jesus' Name."

After this, my pain subsided significantly for a short period of time. It flared up again, and Steve rebuked Satan once more. Again, the pain faded for a while. This went on for several days. We honestly did not know if the changes in pain were a "natural" thing or caused by the rebuking. If it was the rebuking, why did the pain come back? We remembered the words of the visiting pastor, "Rebuke the devil WHENEVER he comes around." We were learning how to engage in active "spiritual warfare!"

I started doing this on my own when Steve was at work. I would read Scripture aloud and tell Satan to flee from me in Jesus' Name.

I said what Jesus said:

> *"Away from me, Satan! For it is written: 'Worship the Lord your God, and serve him only!"*
> Matthew 4:10 (NIV)

Submit yourselves, then, to God. Resist the devil, and he
will flee from you.
James 4:7 (NIV)

You belong to your father, the devil, and you want to carry
out your father's desires. He was a murderer from the
beginning, not holding to the truth, for there is no truth in
him. When he lies, he speaks his native language, for he is a
liar and the father of lies.
John 8:44 (NIV)

Jesus turned and said to Peter, "Get behind me, Satan!
You are a stumbling block to me; you do not have in
mind the concerns of God, but merely human concerns."
Matthew 16:23 (NIV)

You, dear children, are from God and have overcome
them, because the one who is in you is greater than the
one who is in the world.
1 John 4:4 (NIV)

Beth Is Healed and Her "Why" Gets Answered and Confirmed!

After rebuking Satan, I (Beth) prayed to Jesus for my healing and told the Lord I believed He would heal me. I didn't know when my healing would take place, but I came to believe Jesus had the power to heal me. I was finally starting to know the Light.

My testimony is I was healed by Jesus Christ, and I know that I am loved by God. I was restored and resumed functioning as a wife, mother, daughter, nurse, and more recently, now as a grandmother. I have received from God, and I am volunteering in a healing prayer ministry. Freely I have received, and freely I give. All glory belongs to God, my Deliverer!

A few years after Beth's healing, she was asked to share what happened to her at one of the visiting pastor's healing services. The night before the service, Beth prayed for guidance and went to sleep. In the wee hours of the morning, she woke up and was impressed to focus on the theme "Tell them why it took so long."

In the night, Beth was shown ten concepts she had to understand before she was healed.

1. To believe God loves her. (James 1:17)

2. To believe that God could heal her. She overcame unbelief and hardness of heart. (Mark 16:14)

3. To allow her husband to be her spiritual head. (Ephesians 5:23)

4. To learn that she was in spiritual warfare, and she personally needed to learn how to fight. (1 John 4:4; James 4:7)

5. To know Satan is a liar and the father of lies. She had to replace the lies with the truth. (John 8:44; John 8:33)

6. To know the power of the spoken word of God. (Romans 10:8)

7. To pray for others and get her mind off herself. (James 5:16; Job 42:10)

8. To praise God during suffering. (Psalm 34:1-4)

9. To humble herself and confess her sins before God. (James 5:16)

10. To put to death the old nature. To have a metamorphosis by being transformed by the renewing of her mind. (Colossians 3:9; Philippians 4:8; Romans.12:2; 2 Corinthians 10:5)

God knew exactly what Beth's particular situation was, and He knew what she needed to be healed and thrive long-term. She made the statement that if she would have had a miracle at the first healing service like Steve did with his side; her thought patterns and views of God would have led her back into the same problem.

This is the Word God showed her:

My ears had heard of you but now my eyes have seen you.
Job 42:5 (NIV)

Beth and Steve believed God had shown them "why" it took what they considered to be a long time, but they had never been shown the reason "why" for the exact amount of time. Almost a decade after Beth's talk on "Tell Them Why It Took So Long," Beth and Steve heard Dr. Caroline Leaf speak at their church. (She is a communication pathologist and cognitive neuroscientist specializing in cognitive and metacognitive neuropsychology.) Dr. Leaf, a devout Christian, made the statement that when she was in school, the teaching at that time was that the human brain was hard-wired and could not change.

When Dr. Leaf read the Bible, she found these words:

> *Do not conform to the pattern of this world, but be transformed by the renewing of your mind. Then you will be able to test and approve what God's will is — his good, pleasing and perfect will.*
> Romans 12:2 (NIV)

In her findings, she discovered when a new concept is introduced, it takes twenty-one days for a thought to go from short-term to long-term memory. It then takes two twenty-one-day cycles of ingraining the thought before the brain has rewired itself to recognize the thought as normal.

When they heard three twenty-one-day cycles, Beth and Steve turned and stared at each other. The first service they attended with the visiting pastor was in April. Beth walked out of her dark room on June 14. Beth and Steve were shown by God why it took until June 14 for Beth to be healed. The comments Beth had made years earlier were proven out by scientific facts! Praise be to God![11]

> *I praise you because I am fearfully and wonderfully made; your works are wonderful, I know that full well.*
> Psalm 139:14 (NIV)

Overshadowed by Light — Beth and Steve's Story

ACTS Prayer

Worship Jesus as the Light of the world. Add your prayers in the spaces.

Adoration: Jesus, you are the true light. I worship You because you have given me the true light. I do not walk in darkness, but I walk in your marvelous light.

Confession: I confess that I did not believe You were the true light. I believe now. I want to live as a child of the light.

Thanksgiving: I thank you, Father, that you have given me the fountain of life, Jesus, your only begotten Son. Thank you for saving me.

Supplication: Father, when you created the world, you spoke, and there was light. You saw that the light was good. I ask you to speak life and light to the people in my life, in my State, in my country. Enlighten our darkness. I choose to speak life and not darkness.

Overshadowed by Light — Beth and Steve's Story

Process What You Have Learned

1. What did you learn from Beth and Steve's Testimonies?

2. Have you had to face sickness and disease in your body?

3. What were you taught about healing?

4. What have you been taught about deliverance?

5. What do you believe about healing? Do you know anyone who has been healed?

Overshadowed by Light — Beth and Steve's Story

Biblical Worldview of Healing and Spiritual Warfare

Biblical References

Jesus Healed the Sick — John 6:2; Luke 6:19

Jesus went throughout Galilee, teaching in their synagogues, proclaiming the good news of the kingdom, and healing every disease and sickness among the people.
Matthew 4:23 (NIV)

Jesus went through all the towns and villages, teaching in their synagogues, proclaiming the good news of the kingdom and healing every disease and sickness.
Matthew 9:35 (NIV)

Healing Is For Today — The Prayer Of Faith — James 5:13-16; Psalm 103:1-3

And God has placed in the church first of all apostles, second prophets, third teachers, then miracles, then gifts of healing, of helping, of guidance, and of different kinds of tongues.
1 Corinthians 12:28 (NIV)

We Can Heal As Jesus Healed

Very truly I tell you, whoever believes in me will do the works I have been doing, and they will do even greater things than these, because I am going to the Father.
John 14:12 (NIV)

Healing is in the "The Great Commission" to go and preach the gospel placing hands on the sick.

> *He said to them, "Go into all the world and preach the gospel to all creation. Whoever believes and is baptized will be saved, but whoever does not believe will be condemned. And these signs will accompany those who believe: In my name they will drive out demons; they will speak in new tongues; they will pick up snakes with their hands; and when they drink deadly poison, it will not hurt them at all; they will place their hands on sick people, and they will get well."*
> Mark 16:15-18 (NIV)

Spiritual Warfare — Ephesians 6:10-12; Ephesians 6:13-17

> *The one who does what is sinful is of the devil, because the devil has been sinning from the beginning. The reason the Son of God appeared was to destroy the devil's work.*
> 1 John 3:8 (NIV)

> *Submit yourselves, then, to God. Resist the devil, and he will flee from you.*
> James 4:7 (NIV)

> *And pray in the Spirit on all occasions with all kinds of prayers and requests. With this in mind, be alert and always keep on praying for all the Lord's people.*
> Ephesians 6:18 (NIV)

Chapter Eight
Overshadowed by The Sower — Christie's Testimony

Listen! A farmer went out to sow his seed. As he was scattering the seed, some fell along the path, and the birds came and ate it up. Some fell on rocky places, where it did not have much soil. It sprang up quickly, because the soil was shallow. But when the sun came up, the plants were scorched, and they withered because they had no root. Other seed fell among thorns, which grew up and choked the plants, so that they did not bear grain. Still other seed fell on good soil. It came up, grew and produced a crop, some multiplying thirty, some sixty, some a hundred times."
Mark 4:3-8 (NIV)

My story starts at the beginning in my life when God was planting seeds in my heart. I grew up Catholic, but that was only until I was about eight years old. My parents divorced when I was six years old, and I remember going through the Communion process. However, I did not go to church regularly. Visitation with my father was on Sundays, and he did not take us to church. Occasionally (on Easter, Palm Sunday, Christmas), I went to church with my grandparents. Church-going was not consistent. My mother said little things to give us a bit of a foundation, for example: say a little prayer, love your neighbor, have some patience, respect and honor parents, elders, and authority figures, etc. So, my foundation was limited, but it was there.

Fast forward to my first job out of college, and I land in the Oil Fields of South Texas. My training engineer turns out to be a Southern Baptist man (Kevin), and one of the operators I worked with called himself a "Born Again Christian" (Vince). This is where the seeds of the Gospel of Jesus Christ were planted. Both of these men were placed in my life at this specific time because my life was very pivotal. I was angry

115

with God, but they showed me, love. I was a young woman lost in sin in many aspects. They accepted me for who I was and loved me no matter what, and they became role models. These two men became "the light of God" for me. The seeds of the Gospel were planted, now they were being nourished.

My next job was back in my home state of Michigan. Here the seeds were watered — but I still did not allow them to bear fruit. I started to open my heart. God introduced me to a man who taught me about forgiveness, and he introduced me to "A Higher Power." He showed me that my anger was not with God but just with situations and the effect of growing up in a home with alcoholic and divorced parents. He pointed me to a group that would help me process the anger, guilt, fear, lack of love, and self-esteem issues. This is where the seeds were really fertilized. The group helped me to accept (love the person and not the sin), to forgive, and to ask God for help. The man was a great friend and mentor through this process. He showed me how much he loved the Lord and how God helped turn his life around. Three years after I started this process, we became husband and wife. The seed was being watered and cared for during this process; still, I resisted the harvest.

I continued to walk through issues at my pace, and that is where God decided I needed a jolt. I had been married for five years, had a three-year-old son, and was pregnant with another. My husband was having medical issues and was on short-term disability. Our savings account was running low. I had a friend at work named Marie who came alongside of me. The first time we spoke, we laughed together.

Marie: Hi, I'm Marie. I met Christie at my new job as a Sales Support Representative in the Automotive industry. I was a stay-at-home mom for fourteen years and worked as a Christian school teacher for sixteen years. This new job made me feel like a fish out of water as I entered the building of Corporate America on my first day at work and made my way

116

to a cubicle. I had computer/office skills, so the job wasn't difficult. I didn't know anyone, and I passed right by Christie's desk every morning. She was pregnant, and so was my daughter, so we had some common ground for conversation. Christie was very likable. I saw her as very intelligent — she was an engineer — I admired that. She made me laugh as she educated me on how engineers think differently, and they are prone to analyze and process things from every single angle. I did not have a brain like that, but in no time at all, we became friends.

Christie: One morning, my friend, Marie, gave me a KJV Bible (King James Version), which I could not read and had to return it lovingly. She then gave me an NIV, (New International Version) which I understood, but the reading was still difficult. At Christmastime, I was blessed with "The Picture Bible," which I not only understood but read through in its entirety in two weeks.

Marie: One morning as I went by Christie's desk at work, I gave her a Bible. It happened to be a King James Version. I didn't think anything of it until a few days later when she gave the Bible back to me. "The 'thee's' and 'thou's' are just not working for me," she said.

"No problem," I said.

The next day I brought her a New International Version. That version seemed to fit Christie better. One of the ways the Lord speaks to us is through the Bible, and it's important to have a version that suits us in a personal way. *The Picture Bible* was so relevant to me when I first got saved. I would read it to my children. Because the Old Testament was hard for me to grasp, *The Picture Bible* made it come to life. I always recommend it to new believers who have children, and, of course, I urged Christie to read it. I liked the fact that I learned at the same time as my children as we read it together every day. There is a new version called *The Action Bible* that I have given to all my grandchildren, and the artwork is incredible!

Christie: Marie was a light in my life, and yet, I was still not reaching out to turn the light on. She continued to be a friend, introduced me to her daughter, and we spent one night a month just getting together and doing some crafts—a "Mom's night out." After a few events, I realized that most of these women went to church together—none of them pushed church or God on me; they all just kept bringing more light into my life.

> *Listen then to what the parable of the sower means: When anyone hears the message about the kingdom and does not understand it, the evil one comes and snatches away what was sown in their heart. This is the seed sown along the path. The seed falling on rocky ground refers to someone who hears the word and at once receives it with joy. But since they have no root, they last only a short time. When trouble or persecution comes because of the word, they quickly fall away. The seed falling among the thorns refers to someone who hears the word, but the worries of this life and the deceitfulness of wealth choke the word, making it unfruitful. But the seed falling on good soil refers to someone who hears the word and understands it. This is the one who produces a crop, yielding a hundred, sixty or thirty times what was sown."*
> Matthew 13:18-23 (NIV)

Marie: Christie chides that I "hounded" her, but I say I "shared" with her. I cared about her as a person. We invited her to join our craft group, where we laughed and enjoyed an evening devoid of problems and work issues. We met at my daughter's condo. I was thrilled that my daughter and her family had moved back to Michigan from Florida. Laurie was pregnant with her third child, Natalia. As we were working, I introduced Christie to my son-in-law, who passed through the dining room—it was a quick introduction.

Christie: Then, it all came crashing down on me. When God wants to get my attention, He knows I have to be hit hard. I just had a baby, my husband experienced a seizure, Grandma had heart surgery, my uncle died, my mother-in-law had surgery, then my husband had a second seizure, and my mother was experiencing health issues as well. This all happened within the space of six weeks. Needless to say, I was a bundle of stress, but I was determined that I could still manage on my own. It wasn't until I got through a couple more events that I finally started to look at churches. My friend at work continued to pray, and I found myself in her cubicle asking if it would be OK to attend church with her. And here is where my walk with Jesus started.

Marie: "You're asking to go to church with us?" I said. "Yes, of course. Are you kidding?"

God was drawing Christie to Jesus because His desire was to overshadow her with His mercy and goodness. The Christian women who gathered for crafts had no idea what trials Christie would be facing in her marriage and family life. Christie sat with us on her first Sunday attending our church. We sat up front in the second row. It's hard to describe to someone how wonderfully joy-filled our church services are, so I didn't say much to prepare Christie. My son-in-law was the Worship Arts pastor who she had just met at their condo with a five-second "Hi, how are you?" She glanced up and saw him at the keyboard singing and did a double take. Is this the same regular guy she just met when the ladies were crafting together?

Marie: To describe the praise and worship in church that morning as "lively" would be an understatement. After a few songs, Christie leaned over and whispered in my ear: "This church rocks!" I laughed…in church. What a fun moment it was for all of us (friends) to see her take it all in and experience LIFE and JOY bursting forth in her innermost being…in a church service.

I would not have described our church by saying, "Christie, come to my church; it rocks!" The way she phrased her first reaction to church that morning was pure joy for me! We still laugh about that, too!

Christie: I started to attend church with my friend at Auburn Hills Christian Center. I worshipped God, felt His presence, and understood the messages Pastor Cal gave. I started to watch "Veggie Tales" to understand the Bible. I was a baby Christian but a hungry one. I continued to learn about Jesus and the Father, His Word, and how to worship Him. My faith was growing, and I thank God for that time of foundational building. I didn't know it, but this growth would sustain me in the near future.

Christie: During this time of faith-building, my husband, Zane, continued to battle with medical issues. He struggled with prescription medications and a diagnosis that could be treated but not cured. The treatment for this diagnosis? More prescription drugs! He started the "Medication Hop" and just went from one to another over the course of a couple of years. I had my suspicions that he was abusing the drugs, and that is when he would switch it up. Zane was very clever! I was learning to listen to the Lord through my heart and started to find evidence of the abuse. I had to confront him. Zane had to make a choice because our marriage and our family life were crumbling. He chose to go to rehab, and he was drug free at this point.

Marie: I saw the faithfulness of God as Christie walked through this difficult situation with her husband. At one point, Christie was led by the Lord out to her garage to a stash of drugs her husband had hidden there. Christie was learning to hear God's voice! This is foundational to the Christian life, and so many people don't know they can hear God's voice! I saw how much God cared about Christie and Zane and their two boys. This great love was unfolding before my eyes!

The Lord is a refuge for the oppressed, a stronghold in
times of trouble.
Psalm 9:9 (NIV)

Christie: It was during this time that my relationship with
God was strengthened. I dug deep into the Bible, continued to
go to mentoring meetings, and was blessed with not only one
great mentor – but three! Every single one of these women
taught me and mentored me in ways that only God could
direct. He gave me friends and "spiritual moms" to help me
through everyday life and its challenges. ["Spiritual mom" is a
term used to describe an older woman who comes alongside a
younger woman to help her grow in her walk with the Lord
with prayer and encouragement.]

Marie: Christie and I joined a mentoring group at our church.
We went to monthly meetings together. We did Bible studies
during lunch. Sometimes, we just walked at noon and chatted.
These were special times for both of us. After a year or two
went by, new mentors were chosen. The purpose of changing
is to broaden the mentee's perspective in relationships with
many women. Every woman has her own faith walk and
diverse gifts of the Spirit. The new believer needs to see the
various ways women walk out their faith. Many other women
came alongside Christie and provided friendship, too. She was
easy to love.

Likewise, teach the older women to be reverent in the
way they live, not to be slanderers or addicted to much
wine, but to teach what is good. Then they can urge the
younger women to love their husbands and children, to
be self-controlled and pure, to be busy at home, to be
kind, and to be subject to their husbands, so that no one
will malign the word of God.
Titus 2:3-5 (NIV)

Christie: My husband was diagnosed as permanently
medically disabled, and he stopped working. While he
received some long-term benefits, it was not the same as a

paycheck. Our boys were in elementary school now, and my husband gave the boys after-school care. He helped around the house with meals, laundry, and shopping, but without the accountability of a job, his addictive nature started to resurface once again.

Right before the economic downturn, our investment portfolio started to suffer. Instead of us just riding out the wave (we were still 20 years from retiring), Zane withdrew his 401K and found the local "Club Keno," and other gambling stops. While we had to pay taxes, we did not have to pay any penalties because of his medical condition. The IRS saw that as one of the extenuating circumstances to do an early withdrawal. Zane wanted to keep the portfolio growing and not see the losses that happen when you invest. It was late 2008 when he finally told me of this situation, and we owed the IRS money. I was devastated that the man I loved went behind my back and gambled our money away. We had been through drug addictions, medical issues, and now gambling. I was frustrated, angry, disappointed, and hurt…and yes, abandoned. The trust I had in our relationship was disappearing. I tried to look to God, but I still felt darkness surround me.

Then 2009 came, I was laid off from my job. I struggled as I wanted to leave my husband and start over. At the same time, I felt the Lord telling me this time of being laid off would be a time for rebuilding a broken relationship. My husband, once again, wanted to do what was best, but he did it the wrong way. He started to gamble more. Over the next year, he slowly liquidated my 401K, the college fund for the kids, and the investment portfolio. All of this was done without me knowing as I never got the mail, never saw any account balances, and I wanted to believe that we were rebuilding. I was able to get a new job within five months of being laid off — God was at work. I dug deeper into God and looked for guidance, wisdom, peace, and faith. I was searching for the light in my darkness and still unaware that my husband was lying and stealing.

Marie: Christie was such a blessing. She began to be actively involved in nursery ministry. Because of the downturn in the economy, our church began to hold prayer meetings on Wednesday nights. The pastor knew that many people were struggling in financial areas. This prayer meeting still exists because we saw the powerful changes that came because of prayer. Our church prayed for Christie and Zane. The State of Michigan was devastated during this economic downturn. The pastor arranged a special dinner and invited all those who were laid-off or struggling with their mortgages, loss of employment, etc. The dinner was a bright spot and brought great encouragement for many in the church. The families knew someone cared about them personally. They needed a touch of hope.

Christie: My world started to fall apart in July 2011. The IRS called my place of work, instructing the payroll department to garnish my wages. I was notified that the garnishment was going to take place in my next paycheck. This is when I found out we owed the government, and we were not paying the bills. I was devastated and extremely embarrassed. We had been fighting potential foreclosure on our home, and now I was faced with the government taking roughly 50 percent of my paycheck. This is when I found out that my husband had continued to gamble.

Marie: I knew Christie's boss and saw how he helped in every way he could during this garnishment of Christie's wages. One day I saw her boss in a restaurant and I thanked him for helping Christie. He said the same thing to me, "Thanks for helping Christie." We felt a mutual bond that day. I respected him for helping the way he could as her boss. He respected the way I was able to help with encouragement on the spiritual side. God works through people. He equips us in different ways to help people. As Christie struggled through this trial, we (the church) wanted her to be spared the distress of it all, but only God can bring a person THROUGH a trial. We saw our Heavenly Father love Christie through all of this trouble as we continued to pray for His goodness upon her and her family.

Christie: In December 2011, we were served a foreclosure notice on our home and had to be out by June. I thought Zane would realize he was driving the family into poverty. I was wrong. He was addicted and longed for the quick fix to all of our financial problems. Over the next six months, I attempted to build up my bank account. I worked with the IRS to set up a payment plan, so that I could still provide a home and food for my kids. After six months, I figured out I was living paycheck to paycheck, not getting anywhere, and devastated to see the kids' accounts were being liquidated. It was at this point I determined enough was enough. I told my husband that the boys and I were moving out of the home we were losing, and he was not coming with us. I determined that a marriage separation was the best thing for us. I told him that I would not file for a divorce, so he was covered on my insurance, but I also told him that he had to get help.

Bills continued to come in; there were collection agencies chasing me for money on credit cards I did not even know I had. My credit rating hit the lowest it could possibly go, and I struggled to get into an apartment because they wanted six months' rent upfront. I borrowed money from my mother and asked my church for help. I had a plan to start over, and it did not include my husband. With all my assets protected, the kids and I moved into an apartment. My husband moved into a different apartment. I had a budget, and we lived within the budget, with monthly deposits coming in from my husband to pay for the tax bills. I started to save money for college and retirement but still had a sense of darkness. I prayed every day, went to the altar every weekend, cried out to God for help, and pressed into His Word.

He cuts off every branch in me that bears no fruit, while every branch that does bear fruit he prunes so that it will be even more fruitful.
John 15:2 (NIV)

Christie: I was on the mend and was looking into filing for divorce as I did not see Zane getting help or changing. I realized the only option I had was to sever the relationship. However, when I went to visit my husband, I knew things were not quite right, and I questioned him about his health — what was truly going on and how I could help? He was adamant that he was fine; he said his weight loss was due to him trying to get in shape. After eighteen months of separation from his family and with a decrease in his weight, my husband passed away at the age of fifty-two due to liver failure — he had gone back to drinking, which ultimately took his life. Before he died, my sons went to visit Zane in his apartment, and had a heart-to-heart talk with him, and prayed with their dad.

Marie: We came alongside Christie as she walked through the death of her husband. Zane's funeral was held at our church. Many of our work associates came. Women of the church helped Christie cleanout Zane's apartment and were with her, literally, helping in any way they could. That is what the family of God, the Church, is supposed to look like in the world today. "A very present help in times of trouble." We are the Lord's hands and feet.

Christie: Now, I was faced with further darkness. What once was hopeful (a mended relationship) was now totally gone. My best friend died. I was a "widow" at age forty-five, with two kids in school (ages 16 and 12), and the government was not letting up on any of my bills. My first hurdle was to pay off the State Tax bill. The small life insurance policy I had through my job was just enough to cover that bill: one bill down, one huge one to conquer. I continued to save, invest, and pay the bill. There were ups and downs. I attempted to get relief from the government because I did not know about the withdrawal of the 401K immediately. Unfortunately, spouses are only given two years to file that claim—I was well into year three when I started the process. So, I continued to save and press into God—asking for favor and guidance. I let Him lead me to a point where I started to look at retirement at a regular age, a college fund for my children, and newer transportation.

Now faith is confidence in what we hope for and assurance about what we do not see.
Hebrews 11:1 (NIV)

As the years went by, I grew in faith. Faith is action and risk, and it all culminated on a Sunday morning in church in October 2016. I wanted to get out of my apartment. I was considering a rent-to-own idea. A friend at church was willing to help me since I could not get a mortgage with an open tax bill. I sat on these thoughts for six weeks. Pastor Cal did what he always does when the sermon was finished—he called us up to the altar to pray. As I had done on numerous occasions, I went up to the altar. I heard God speak to me! It was so loud; I actually looked around to see who may have said the words. All I saw were people around me praying, and then I knew it was God. He said three simple words: "PAY THE BILL." I went home and looked at my investments, my 401K, and my savings. I did multiple calculations and realized I could pay off the government and not set myself back for retirement. So it was, in November 2016, I took out a small loan against my 401K and paid off the government. I was free of the IRS! I started looking at homes I could afford, and within six months, I became the proud owner of a two-story colonial—the kids each had their own room!

I look back on the last 16 years, and I thank God for introducing me to Marie at work, the one who led me to Christ. I thank Him for the path He led me down, for speaking to me quietly and gently and through different people. For His faithfulness and patience with me because fifteen years ago, I was a baby Christian. Five years ago, I was in such deep darkness, and I knew God, and His love surrounded me. Where I am today can only be attributed to the Glory of God. The verse that carried me through the last seven years was Jeremiah 29:11 — I know God has plans for me. I hung on to that every day, and HE pulled me through. God's promises can be trusted. The planted seeds are producing fruit…and the seed fell on good ground.

> Then Jesus said to them, "Don't you understand this parable? How then will you understand any parable? The farmer sows the word. Some people are like seed along the path, where the word is sown. As soon as they hear it, Satan goes and takes away the word that was sown in them. Others, like seed sown on rocky places, hear the word and at once receive it with joy. But since they have no root, they last only a short time. When trouble or persecution comes because of the word, they quickly fall away. Still others, like seed sown among thorns, hear the word; but the worries of this life, the deceitfulness of wealth and the desires for other things come in and choke the word, making it unfruitful. Others, like seed grown on good soil, hear the word, accept it, and produce a crop — some thirty, some sixty, some a hundred times what was sown."
>
> Mark 4:13-20 (NIV)

Overshadowed by The Sower — Christie's Testimony

ACTS Prayer

Worship the Sower who gave us the Word of God and write your prayers.

Adoration: I love you, Lord, because you have brought me through so many things. I could not have come through without you. I worship you as my God, my refuge, my fortress, my deliverer. You are my Faithful Father God.

Confession: I repent of not always seeing you in the dark times of my life. I see that you didn't mean trials to harm me, but you were building faith in me and what the enemy meant for evil, You turned for good. I confess that I didn't always have a good attitude in these times. I confess that I didn't trust that You would come through for me. You did. You always do.

Thanksgiving: Thank you for loving me when I didn't even know You. Thank you for your mercy and grace in my life. Thank you for the foundation of faith you formed in my heart...a strong foundation.

Supplication: I pray that you will bring my boys to the saving knowledge of Jesus Christ. You did it for me, Lord. Draw them to you. Build a solid foundation in them so that they can stand when the trials of life come into their lives. Show them who You are.

Overshadowed by The Sower—Christie's Testimony

Process What You Have Learned

1. What did you learn from Christie's Testimony?

2. Do you have people with addictions in your life?

3. What are some of the circumstances in your life that you would like to see God change?

4. Was anything in this testimony similar to your life?

5. Did any one thing stand out to you as you read Christie's testimony?

Overshadowed by The Sower — Christie's Testimony

Biblical Worldview Of Trouble

◆ Jesus told us in this world, we will have trouble. (tribulation)
◆ The Bible has answers when life overwhelms us.
◆ Jesus experienced being sorrowful and troubled.

Biblical References:

Trouble

Blessed are those who mourn for they shall be comforted.
Matthew 5:4 (NIV)

Therefore do not worry about tomorrow, for tomorrow will worry about itself. Each day has enough trouble of its own.
Matthew 6:34 (NIV)

But since they have no root, they last only a short time. When trouble or persecution comes because of the word, they quickly fall away.
Matthew 13:21 (NIV)

I have been born of God and I overcome the world. This is the victory that has overcome the world, even our faith.
1 John 5:4 (NIV)

Who is it that overcomes the world? Only the one who believes that Jesus is the Son of God.
1 John 5:5 (NIV)

Chapter Nine
Overshadowed in Suffering — Corrie ten Boom's Testimony

"I do not want my children to see this movie!" exclaimed the irate mother to the teacher. "I don't believe in suffering, and I will not expose my children to it. When you show it in your classroom, I will keep them home that day!"

I was surprised at this mother's reaction. Of course, she had the freedom to choose to keep her children home, but can we deny suffering is a part of life? Can we deny evil exists? This experience happened when I taught in a Christian school many years ago. I showed the movie *The Hiding Place* to my upper elementary class. Corrie ten Boom wrote the book by the same title, and the movie was launched a few years later. Can we shield our children from suffering? Should we?

The true story of Corrie ten Boom shows how one family had to decide how to live their lives during a period of history where heinous leaders inflicted great evil on an entire race of people. The ten Boom family decided to save people one at a time. What action can we take when we are presented with evil? We see examples of bravery, sacrifice, and compassion.

The Hiding Place is a World War II story of a middle-aged woman, Corrie ten Boom, who lived in Holland with her family. Casper ten Boom, Corrie's father, a widower, owned a watch shop, and the family home was attached to shop. Corrie and her sister Betsie were single women who helped their elderly father. In 1922, following in her father's footsteps, Corrie studied and became the first woman licensed as a watchmaker in Holland. All of the family were strong Christians, and they put their faith into action whenever they could. When the Nazis began persecuting the Jews, the ten Boom family did all they could to support the Jews. The family became part of the Dutch resistance. Some accounts say that Corrie and her family helped save eight hundred lives, including Jewish babies.

One day, a man whom Corrie trusted, who happened to be a Dutch informant, betrayed the ten Boom family. At the time, the family was hiding six Jews in their home to shelter them from persecution and death. The ten Booms were arrested, but the Jews were not found by the soldiers. Three days later, the Jews escaped unharmed from their hiding place in the ten Boom home. They were able to slip away without being discovered by the police, who had been watching the house.

Corrie's father, 84, died in prison. Corrie and her sister Betsie endured much suffering at the hands of the cruel Nazi guards in a concentration camp. Betsie and Corrie were able to comfort many prisoners as they shared the Word of God and led them to salvation in Jesus Christ. How would the guards ever allow that? Fleas? Lice? The women's barracks had an infestation, and the guards wanted no part of it, so they did not enter the barracks. Corrie confessed to Betsie that she couldn't thank God for the pests. Betsie reminded Corrie how God could take bad things that happen to us and make them work toward good in our lives. The insects allowed the sisters to tell the prisoners of Jesus' great love. The result: rescue and salvation happening in a concentration camp! God's ways are past finding out, and His mercies are new every morning!

Corrie and Betsie had to forgive the cruelties they witnessed and endured. They found Jesus' love to be much greater than any darkness in the horrible death camps. Betsie died in the concentration camp. Her sister's death was very difficult and painful for Corrie. God had allowed them to be together in the prison, but now Betsie was gone, and Corrie was feeling terrible loneliness. Corrie thought that she and her sister would travel the world together. Corrie had to receive the comfort that only God could give her. Ninety-seven thousand women were killed in the prison where Corrie and her sister were taken.

After Corrie was released from prison, she learned that her release was due to a clerical error.

A week later, the women Corrie's age were executed — all sent to the gas chambers. God had more Kingdom work for Corrie to do. She became an evangelist, and God sent her all over the world preaching the Gospel of Jesus Christ. Corrie testified to the power of God's love, the amazing gift of God's forgiveness, and the importance of forgiving others. Forgiveness causes the peace of God to reside in our hearts.

I have read Corrie's story many times, over and over through the years. As I visualize the Lord overshadowing Corrie's life, I am fascinated with the dangers, the adversities, the choices, the miracles she experienced before, during, and after incarceration in the dreaded death camps. Even when we are confronted with extreme conditions, God asks us to forgive everyone, even our enemies. She forgave the cruelest of guards. She recovered from this horrible ordeal. There is power in Corrie's testimony. God's way everyday!

Corrie gave her testimony as she traveled around the world. The death camps were hell on earth, and God enabled her to survive the worst of circumstances. She preached the Gospel in prisons. Corrie knew what it felt like to be a prisoner.

She preached in churches wherever she was invited from Vietnam to Israel to the USA, crisscrossing the globe to more than sixty countries. Following is one of the testimonies from Corrie ten Boom when she had a speaking engagement in a church in Germany.

I'm Still Learning to Forgive — Corrie ten Boom

"It was in a church in Munich where I was speaking in 1947 that I saw him — a balding heavyset man in a gray overcoat, a brown felt hat clutched between his hands. One moment I saw the overcoat and brown hat; the next, a blue uniform and a visored cap with its skull and crossbones.

"Memories of the concentration camp came back with a rush: the huge room with its arch overhead lights, the pathetic pile of dresses and shoes in the center of the floor, the shame of walking naked past this man. I could see my sister's frail form ahead of me, ribs sharp beneath the parchment of skin.

Betsie and I had been arrested for concealing Jews in our home during the Nazi occupation of Holland. This man had been a guard at Ravensbruck concentration camp where we were sent.

Now he was in front of me, hand thrust out: "A fine message, fräulein! How good it is to know that, as you say, all our sins are at the bottom of the sea!" It was the first time since my release that I had been face to face with one of my captors, and my blood seemed to freeze.

"You mentioned Ravensbruck in your talk," he was saying. "I was a guard there. But since that time," he went on, "I have become a Christian. I know that God has forgiven me for the cruel things I did there, but I would like to hear it from your lips as well. Fraulein—" again the hand came out—"will you forgive me?"

And I stood there—and could not. Betsie had died in that place—could he erase her slow terrible death simply for the asking?

"It could not have been many seconds that he stood there, hand held out, but to me it seemed hours as I wrestled with the most difficult thing I had ever had to do."

"For I had to do it—I knew that. The message that God forgives has a prior condition: that we forgive those who have injured us. "If you do not forgive men their trespasses," Jesus says, "neither will your Father in Heaven forgive your trespasses."

"Still, I stood there with the coldness clutching my heart. But forgiveness is an act of the will, and the will can function regardless of the temperature of the heart. "Jesus help me!" I prayed silently. "I can lift my hand. I can do that much. You supply the feeling."

"And so woodenly, mechanically, I thrust my hand into the one stretched out to me. And as I did, an incredible thing took place. The current started in my shoulder, raced down my arm, sprang into our joined hands. And then this healing warmth seemed to flood my whole being, bringing tears to my eyes."

"I forgive you, brother!" I cried. "With all my heart!"

For a long moment we grasped each other's hands, the former guard and former prisoner. I had never known God's love so intensely as I did then.

With Corrie's willingness came God's power to forgive her former captor.[12]

Corrie's Quotes on Forgiveness

"Forgiveness is an act of the will, and the will can function regardless of the temperature of the heart."

"This is what the past is for!"

"And for all these people alike, the key to healing turned out to be the same. Each had a hurt he had to forgive."

"Forgiveness is the key that unlocks the door of resentment and the handcuffs of hatred.

It is a power that breaks the chains of bitterness and the shackles of selfishness."

Corrie ten Boom

Jesus said "Follow Me." The disciples each had to decide whether they would say "Yes" to that invitation. Was there suffering because they answered "Yes?" What kind of world would we have if everyone said: "Yes to God?" You can see God gave us a free will. He wants people to love Him because they decide to love Him. God does not force people to love Him. If force is used, it isn't love or freedom. Corrie had many days when she decided to love and obey God. There are many people in eternity with Jesus because Corrie said "Yes to God" time after time in her life. Her testimony presents a mural of faith, courage and resilience, and hope, and after her recovery, she brought Jesus' abundant life wherever He asked her to go.

Books by Corrie ten Boom:

The Hiding Place
    Prison Letters
      Tramp for the Lord
        In My Father's House

Movie: The Hiding Place

Marching Orders for the End Battle
A Prisoner and Yet
Plenty for Everyone
Common Sense Not Needed
Not Good if Detached
Oh How He Loves You
I Stand at the Door and Knock

Overshadowed in Suffering — Corrie ten Boom's Testimony

ACTS Prayer

Add your prayers in the spaces and worship the God who sees your suffering. Read the Biblical Worldview of Suffering at the end of this chapter.

Adoration: I worship you in my time of suffering. You don't bring sickness and disease, but You have told us that we would go through things in this life. You are omniscient, and you have all the answers we need.

Confession: I choose to trust you, Lord. Thank you for forgiving me time after time after time.

Thanksgiving: Thank you for drawing me to you. I bow before you.

Supplication: I will tell of all your deeds — reign over my family, friends, work associates.

Overshadowed in Suffering — Corrie ten Boom's Testimony

Process What You Have Read

1. What suffering have you endured in your life?

2. What has been the worst day of your life? How did you get through these times?

3. Have you forgiven people in your life?

4. Corrie lived in an evil time when Nazi Germany exterminated millions of people. Do you think her story is relevant today? Why or why not?

5. Did Corrie give you a perspective that you have not thought of before? What applies to your life?

Overshadowed in Suffering—Corrie ten Boom's Testimony

Biblical Worldview Of Suffering

◆ Jesus suffered. Our Savior knows our human sufferings, and He has compassion for us. You are engraved on the Lord's hand.

◆ God helps us in our suffering.

◆ Jesus warned we would have tribulation.

◆ The "Last Days" are described for us in the Bible.

The Bible verses below teach us about suffering. Strong's Concordance G2346 gives us the New Testament Greek word *thlipsis*, meaning tribulation. The word tribulation is described as a pressing, pressing together, pressure; in biblical and ecclesiastical writings, tribulation is a Greek metaphor meaning oppression, affliction, distress, straits.

Biblical References:

Jesus Suffered — Hebrews 2:9-10; Philippians 3:10

> *He was despised and rejected by men, a man of sorrows and acquainted with grief; and as one from whom men hide their faces he was despised, and we esteemed him not. Surely he has borne our griefs and carried our sorrows; yet we esteemed him stricken, smitten by God, and afflicted. But he was pierced for our transgressions; he was crushed for our iniquities; upon him was the chastisement that brought us peace, and with his wounds we are healed.*
> Isaiah 53:3-5 (ESV)

And he said to them, "My soul is very sorrowful, even to death. Remain here and watch." And going a little farther, he fell on the ground and prayed that, if it were possible, the hour might pass from him. And he said, "Abba, Father, all things are possible for you. Remove this cup from me. Yet not what I will, but what you will."
Mark 14:34-36 (ESV)

God Helps Us In Our Suffering — Isaiah 49:13-16; Psalm 25:2

Be gracious to me, O God, be gracious and merciful to me, for my soul finds shelter and safety in You, and in the shadow of Your wings I will take refuge and be confidently secure until destruction passes by.
Psalm 57:1 (AMP)

Jesus Warned We Would Have Tribulation — Romans 8:18; James 5:10; 1 Peter 4:13

[Jesus] I have said these things to you, that in me you may have peace. In the world you will have tribulation. But take heart; I have overcome the world."
John 16:33 (ESV)

The Last Days Suffering — Matthew 24:9-14; Matthew 24:15-21

"But watch yourselves lest your hearts be weighed down with dissipation and drunkenness and cares of this life, and that day come upon you suddenly like a trap. For it will come upon all who dwell on the face of the whole earth. But stay awake at all times, praying that you may have strength to escape all these things that are going to take place, and to stand before the Son of Man."
Luke 21:34-36 (ESV)

But the Holy Spirit tells us clearly that in the last times some in the church will turn away from Christ and become eager followers of teachers with devil-inspired ideas. These teachers will tell lies with straight faces and do it so often that their consciences won't even bother them.
1 Timothy 4:1-2 (TLB)

You may as well know this too, Timothy, that in the last days it is going to be very difficult to be a Christian. For people will love only themselves and their money; they will be proud and boastful, sneering at God, disobedient to their parents, ungrateful to them, and thoroughly bad. They will be hardheaded and never give in to others; they will be constant liars and troublemakers and will think nothing of immorality. They will be rough and cruel, and sneer at those who try to be good. They will betray their friends; they will be hotheaded, puffed up with pride, and prefer good times to worshiping God. They will go to church, yes, but they won't really believe anything they hear. Don't be taken in by people like that.
2 Timothy 3:1-5 (TLB)

Wait

by Russell Kelfer

Desperately, helplessly, longingly, I cried;
Quietly, patiently, lovingly God replied.
I pled and I wept for a clue to my fate
And the Master so gently said, "Wait."

"Wait? You say, wait?" my indignant reply.
"Lord, I need answers. I need to know why!
Is your hand shortened? Or have you not heard?
By faith I have asked, and I'm claiming your Word.

"My future and all to which I relate
Hangs in the balance, and you tell me to wait?
I'm needing a 'yes,' a go-ahead sign,
Or even a 'no' to which I can resign.
"You promised, dear Lord, that if we believe,
We need but to ask, and we shall receive.
And Lord, I've been asking, and this is my cry:
I'm weary of asking! I need a reply!"

Then quietly, softly, I learned of my fate
As my Master replied again, "Wait."
So, I slumped in my chair, defeated and taut,
and grumbled to God, "So, I'm waiting for what?

He seemed then to kneel, and His eyes met with mine...
and He tenderly said, "I could give you a sign.
I could shake the heavens and darken the sun.
I could raise the dead and cause mountains to run."

"I could give all you seek and pleased you would be.
You'd have what you want, but you wouldn't know Me.
You'd not know the depth of my love for each saint.
You'd not know the power that I give to the faint."

"You'd not learn to see through the clouds of despair;
You'd not learn to trust just by knowing I'm there.
You'd not know the joy of resting in Me
When darkness and silence are all you can see."

You'd never experience that fullness of love
When the peace of My Spirit descends like a dove.
You would know that I give, and I save, for a start,
But you'd not know the depth of the beat of My heart."

"The glow of My comfort late into the night,
The faith that I give when you walk without sight.
The depth that's beyond getting just what you ask
From an infinite God who makes what you have last."

"You'd never know, should your pain quickly flee,
What it means that My grace is sufficient for thee.
Yes, your dearest dreams overnight would come true,
But, oh, the loss, if you missed what I'm doing in you."

"So, be silent, my child, and in time you will see
That the greatest of gifts is to truly know me.
And though oft My answers seem terribly late,
My most precious answer of all is still…Wait."[13]

Can you sense the Lord overshadowing you when you read this poem? Are you able to hear God's love for you? Isn't our God awesome? He knows just what we need and when.

We are learning in these difficult days that our magnificent Creator hears and answers ALL of our prayers. The Sovereign God responds to our prayers in three ways: YES, NO, and WAIT.

I have admired Russel Kelfer's way of awakening this truth. God whispers: you must trust!

Wait is one of my favorite poems. I have had it so long I don't remember when the poem came my way. I vaguely remember getting it as a fax from someone. As a schoolteacher, I would tell my students, "always sign your work," and I would use the example of the "Wait" poem because, at the bottom of my printed copy, it said: "Author unknown."

As I read the poem, I wondered: Who penned these words that, in some instances, were my exact thoughts? Who is reading my mind? The poem has a perspective that helped me get to the other side of many trials, sufferings, and losses, including mysteries where God thinks so differently from mere humans. I have read and reread the poem many times and passed it on to many people who I knew needed encouragement.

I did some research and was delighted to find there is an author for this poem! He did sign his work! The author is Russell Lee Kelfer, born in San Antonio, Texas, in 1933. He became a minister of the Gospel of Jesus Christ and taught for many years on the radio. He wrote twenty-two poems and used the poems when he preached the Word of God. I was amused to find this little quip from a congregant: "Oh, my dear. Three points and a poem again? Really?" I am sure the people missed his style when he passed on in the year 2000 at the age of 66.

One of Russell's poems entitled "You Are Who You Are For a Reason" was included in Rick Warren's book, *The Purpose Driven Life,* published in 2002. The book sold over 50 million copies in more than 85 languages by 2020. That poem circled the globe!

Chapter Ten
Overshadowed by God's Sovereignty — Drew's Story

"Mom, Jessie's in labor." I heard my oldest son's voice as I answered my phone.

The date was January 16, 2001. I rushed to Bon Secours Hospital in Gross Point, Michigan.

Months earlier, when our children (Chris, our son, and Jessie, our daughter-in-law) received the results of their first ultrasound, we began to refer to this little one as "Megan, our Valentine Baby." Our pastor's wife had an "everything pink" baby shower at her home, and we joyfully celebrated with family and friends. Now, it seemed she might be arriving four weeks early.

Imagine my surprise when my son came out of the delivery room to where I was waiting and announced, "Jessie had the baby, Mom." He said in an even tone. "And," he added with surprise and excitement in his voice…"It's a boy!" I was surprised and delighted as well.

They named him Andrew Parker and called him Drew. Complications developed. There were breathing issues.

I sat in the waiting room. It's common for some "preemies" to have breathing problems because their lungs aren't fully developed. I reasoned. I went home. I waited for more news. I prayed.

A few days later, another phone call came from Chris: "The doctors are moving Drew to St. John's Hospital. They are telling us that he has some kind of syndrome. He may have only one kidney."

A person can live a long life with one kidney, I reasoned. (Jesse's grandfather lived well into his 80's with one kidney.) I waited. I prayed.

We received another call from our son at 10:30 PM. There was something wrong with Drew's heart, and he was being moved to Children's Hospital in downtown Detroit. Three hospitals. It was one of those calls that you remember where you were exactly when you were told unexpected news. Drew's heart. I remember the call because I was in Dearborn visiting a young teenager I was mentoring. I had just dropped her off at the facility where she was living. I turned the car and headed toward Detroit to meet my husband at the hospital. We wanted to be with our children.

"Drew needs open-heart surgery," the doctors said.

When Drew was five days old, the doctors found multiple heart defects. When he was nine days old, they were planning to do heart surgery, but Drew became too weak, and the doctors were finding other things wrong with him, so surgery was delayed. The news was distressing. I went from praying on my knees to praying on my face toward the floor. I wept before the Lord.

Now, we were in the waiting room on the day of Drew's open-heart surgery. He was five weeks old. He had big, bright, sparkling brown eyes — "button-eyes" is what my dad called them. My husband and I were trying to grasp how a surgeon could perform open-heart surgery on a heart the size of a walnut. The doctor told Chris and Jessie that Drew had a 10 percent chance of making it through the surgery. I went to the hospital chapel and prayed.

"Lord, I ask that Drew would only need this heart surgery. I ask you to heal Drew."

I have been in this place before: a zone of struggle because life has presented a situation that seems too big. This is where my struggle always seemed to land: will God hear my prayer and answer the way I want Him to answer? Will my prayer be effective? I don't want to ask Him the question, "Why?" God has been faithful. He has been good. He is always pouring out grace on us. I chose not to be angry with God, but my prayer sounded like I knew better than God. Then, this whisper came from my heart, "I don't know how to pray, Lord. I don't know how to cope with this."

The Sovereignty Of God

The Sovereignty of God is a topic that is not easily explained. Sovereign is defined as "the supreme authority of a king. God is not subject to any power or law which could be conceived as superior to or other than Himself."[14] The Bible refers to Jesus as the King of Kings and the Lord of Lords. God is not subject to any power or law which could be conceived as superior to or other than Himself. He is omniscient—knowing all things.[15] God rules with great authority from His throne. He is mighty. We use the word omnipotent to describe Him, which means He is all powerful.[16] What does the sovereignty of God mean? God tells us with this verse:

"For My thoughts are not your thoughts, nor are your ways My ways," declares the Lord. "For as the heavens are higher than the earth, so are My ways higher than your ways and My thoughts than your thoughts."
Isaiah 55:8-9 (NASB)

Here are some examples of the great power (sovereignty) of God:

- God gave Pharaoh of Egypt ten chances to repent. Pharaoh considered himself a god, and why should he listen to Moses' God? Pharaoh ordered the killing of Hebrew babies. Pharaoh was a cruel slave master to God's people. Pharaoh would not yield to the plagues that were sent to show him God's power. He would not let the people go to worship God. God hardened Pharaoh's heart. The tenth plague was the death of the firstborn—both people and animals died. Who was greater: Our God or Pharaoh and his false gods?
- Moses led the children of Israel out of Egypt where they were in bondage as slaves. God was with Moses through the plagues, the parting of the Red Sea, and the forty years where they

wandered in the wilderness. It came time for the people to enter the promised land. God did not allow Moses to go in. If Moses represented the Law, was God going to reveal a truth that would unfold at a later time? Who was greater: Moses or God?

- We have to be careful of what we say with our mouths. The Israelites came out of Egypt, but they died in the wilderness because of their complaining and unbelief. Their children were able to go into the promised land, along with Joshua and Caleb went in. Who knew better how to lead the Israelites God through Moses or the people?
- Jesus came to earth in a humble way and was born in a stable. He died on the cross. He is the Son of God. He had to trust His Father's plan to save humanity. We see God triumph when Jesus was resurrected. This was a battle between Satan and Jesus. Who was greater?
- God gives us a choice to believe in Him, but Jesus also told us that no one can come to Him unless the Father grants it. Jesus chooses you. Will you choose Jesus?
- When Jesus comes back, He will come as the King of Kings and Lord of Lords. Evil men will choose to wage war against Jesus. Whose side will you be on: God's side or man's side?

Until we understand God's sovereignty, we will want our own way, and we won't surrender to God's way. We have to learn to trust God. Whose way is better, ours or God's?

We have to resist anger, anxiety, fear, unbelief. We have to resist questioning God. We have to resist giving up on God...because...His ways are far above our ways and His thoughts are far above our thoughts. Unbelief tries to capture us. We need to believe in the sovereign God even when we don't understand.

In the Gospel of John, there is a story of how some of Jesus' disciples were complaining about His teaching in the synagogue. They were offended. These teachings are called "the hard sayings of Jesus."

> *"It is the Spirit who gives life; the flesh provides no benefit; the words that I have   spoken to you are spirit, and are life. But there are some of you who do not believe." For Jesus knew from the beginning who they were who did not believe, and who it was who would betray Him.*
> John 6:63-64 (NASB)

> *As a result of this (what Jesus taught) many of His disciples left, and would no longer walk with Him. So Jesus said to the twelve, "You do not want to leave also, do you?" Simon Peter answered Him, "Lord, to whom shall we go? You have words of eternal life. And we have already believed and have come to know that You are the Holy One of God."*
> John 4:66-69 (NASB)

Some of the disciples "unfollowed" Jesus. They "canceled" Jesus from their lives! Does this sound like our world today? Jesus explained the unbelief that He saw in their hearts. He asked his disciples a question: "Are you going to leave me, too?" Could Jesus be asking me this question in regard to Drew? My response is like Peter: "Lord Jesus, to whom shall I go? You have words of eternal life and I have come to know that you are the Holy One of God."

I realized that I needed to trust in the sovereignty of God concerning Drew.

Knowing God

I returned to the hospital waiting room to the news that Drew's heart surgery had been a success. The two main vessels in the heart were transposed, and the fact that Drew had two holes in his heart actually helped keep him alive. The surgeon switched the two main vessels into their proper positions, rerouted the blood flow, and closed the two openings. The operation took ten hours. We were so thankful to the Lord for bringing our baby boy through the delicate open-heart surgery. What we didn't know was there would be more surgeries…many, many more surgeries. "Help me understand, Lord, "I pray. "I need your peace to walk this out."

Here was a little newborn baby boy that the doctors were trying to classify: "He has CHARGE Syndrome," they said, but Drew didn't have all the conditions that would place him in that diagnosis. So, our children advocated for their baby boy…continually.

Jessie described the details on Drew's Caring Bridge site:

"Hi, I'm Andrew Parker Hall. My parents call me Drew. The doctors say that I have CHARGE syndrome. Each letter stands for a medical condition."

- C: Coloboma of the eye. Many CHARGE syndrome children are born blind. "The diagnosis says I have a coloboma, but I can see!"
- H: Heart defects. "My heart surgery was a success!"
- A: Choanal atresia (narrowing of the passages that go from the nose to the back of the throat). A continuous stream of mucus draining from one or both nostrils could be a sign of an atresia.
- R: Retarded (delayed) growth and development. It also stands for renal, and Drew was born with one kidney. "My great grandpa had one kidney too."
- G: Genitourinary abnormalities. "This is a personal area that we won't talk about, but Mom says, "Rest assured, I'm all boy."

- E: Ears (malformation) a lot of CHARGE syndrome children are born deaf. "My ears look different, but I can hear!"

Chris and Jessie learned what medications worked with Drew, and they learned how to cope with difficult turns in Drew's condition. Crisis situations arose many times. I saw Chris and Jessie persevere and get stronger inwardly. A nurse and I had a conversation when Drew was a few months old. She said, "I have two sons, and they could not handle this. Your son is coping with all of it. He has done well in dealing with Drew's medical condition."

Chris and Jessie knew all the nurses and doctors who cared for Drew. They communicated with them as they walked through multiple emergencies at all times of the day and night. I was very moved in my mother's heart to see the love and care they poured out over their baby boy.

I don't know the exact when or where, but Chris and Jessie said their "Yes to God." They agreed together to trust in the sovereign God. He would overshadow them.

As grandparents, we felt helpless. Our children were faced with very difficult decisions. We could pray. We asked God to give wisdom, physical strength, and courage.

In those early days, when Drew was a newborn, he was in the (NICU) Neonatal Intensive Care Unit. This is a place within the hospital where very sick babies get 24/7 care from teams of doctors and nurses. Some babies stay only a few days; other babies stay for weeks or months.

Drew transferred to the (PICU) Pediatric Intensive Care Unit after his heart surgery. He was in the hospital for four months. He came home on Mother's Day. During his four months stay in the hospital, he had multiple surgeries including cleft palate. The nurses called him "Feisty Drew." He had a fighting spirit that compelled him to persevere.

He started school at the age of three and went until he was eleven. His school had a swimming pool, and I remember going to the pool with Drew one time. He had to have a tracheal tube put in, so swimming was no longer an option for him.

When Drew was five years old, he gained a sister named Emily. When he was eight, he gained a brother named Logan. Em became like Drew's big sister and helped her parents with all his care.

At one point in his development, around the age of seven, he had physical therapy to strengthen his muscles so that he would be able to walk. We were so excited that he was getting this therapy. One day during therapy, however, he suffered a fracture of his femur. Drew's bones had become brittle. This was a difficult turn of events. Drew was then fitted for a wheelchair.

After his spinal fusion, he was in homebound schooling once a week with games or art projects or the teacher read to him and had him answer questions.

As I did my devotions one morning, I came across a Bible verse, and I knew that the Lord was speaking to me about Drew:

> *Take heed that ye despise not one of these little ones; for I say unto you, that in heaven their angels do always behold the face of my Father which is in heaven.*
> Matthew 18:10 (KJV)

I called him my Angel Boy from that time on. When I meditate on this verse, I see the extraordinary truth of how close God is to us. I looked into Drew's face, and Drew's angel looked into the Father's face. That's close! Our faces are called "Imago Dei," meaning the image of God. No wonder we don't like face masks. The "image of God" is covered up!

I used to whisper in Drew's ear: "You are my strong Angel Boy, and you are brave and courageous like King David was." Drew was a giant slayer like David. He faced medical giants.

154

Drew and I communicated heart-to-heart. He wasn't able to talk. He interacted with everyone with his heart. The care-workers/nurses bonded into the family unit and came to love Drew, Emily, and Logan as they helped Chris and Jessie care for Drew. We saw an amazing phenomenon—hearts bonded in love because of a precious special needs boy. How does that happen?

He laughed little giggles, and the giggles shook his shoulders. Drew laughed at puppets, conversations, noises, cartoons like Tom and Jerry; Chris and his goofy noises always got a reaction from Drew; his brother Logan could make him laugh. When Charlie, their dog, came in from being outside, he shook and pranced, and Drew thought this was very funny.

One Christmas, our family celebrated at the Ronald McDonald House in downtown Detroit because Drew had to be admitted to Children's Hospital. I told people that Drew had about forty surgeries, but I lost count. Drew had close to seventy surgeries. We all saw that he was more than a conqueror with a spinal fusion, brain surgeries, shunts put in, shunts taken out. Drew had a brain bleed one time, and I will never forget the shock of the news as we arrived at the hospital. I remember saying to myself: Drew is having brain surgery right now. I had to process the reality as I sat there waiting. We met the neurosurgeon when she came into the waiting room, and she explained how she made "a question mark" incision in Drew's skull and went into the brain to clean up the bleed. She was amazing.

On February 26, 2020, Drew's little heart stopped beating. He was ushered into the presence of Jesus and to his heavenly home. Drew's physical fight was finished. He moved to a place where there is no suffering, no crying, no hospitals, no ambulances, no respirators, no medicines. Heaven is sweeter because Drew is there, and we have a promise that we will see him again.

The timing of Drew's passing showed us that God was with our children. He would over-shadow them in this difficult

155

time. The funeral arrangements were made in advance. Chris and Jessie were advised to make their decisions ahead of time so that the emotional stress would be lessened for them. This turned out to be sound advice.

The celebration of Drew's life took place a week after he passed.

"Grandma, what are we going to do? There's always been three of us," Logan's precious words rent my heart in two. Words are hard to find at moments like these.

We are confident, yes, well pleased rather to be absent from the body and to be present with the Lord.
2 Corinthians 5:8 (NKJV)

God sent His Holy Spirit to comfort us on the day of the funeral. A reunion of former church friends coming to see us was an unexpected surprise…a blessing to all of us. The Body of Christ is a family, and all these people were a part of our lives for many years. You get to thinking that the times you have with a family of believers will never end, but the reality is change is inevitable.

Pastor Joe DePasquale walked with Chris and Jessie throughout Drew's entire life, delivered his funeral message, and brought comfort and closure. We were thankful for his tender words.

After 19 years, we can look back on Drew's life and see that he was a blessing wrapped in the body of a little boy with a myriad of health problems. Blessings aren't always readily recognizable—some are cleverly disguised, and some disguise intricate blessings daunting to unveil.

On the 6th of March, this past Sunday was the anniversary of the disappearance of Flight MH370 on March 8, 2014. One man's story stood out. Because of last-minute work responsibilities, he arrived at the airport late and missed the flight. He shared how irate and upset he was at the inconvenience he was facing. His initial reaction of "how unfair" with accompanying complaints as the story unfolded over pursuant days transitioned to "Why me to be so blessed?" And a humble "to God be the glory."

Another story — a man who wanted to be on the flight, a Jewish man whose travel agent didn't book his clients' travel on the Sabbath. How his annoyance turned to heartfelt gratitude at the turn of events surrounding that doomed flight.

We have stories from Scripture:

•   Jacob lost a son, or so he thought when he sent Joseph to see his brothers and never returned home. Jacob was heartbroken and devastated over the loss, but some twenty-two years later, he found out Joseph was alive! Jacob met and was reunited with Joseph and what was so difficult at first turned out to be a blessing in disguise as his entire family was saved from starvation.

•   There are stories of those who missed flights on 9/11, of those who were late to work at the World Trade Center Towers that day, and so many more.

All to see that blessings are often disguised in packages, life packages, that look like difficulty and delay; they look like hardship and sorrow, but they are blessings nonetheless, revealed over varying lengths and degrees of time.

Not Cheated By His Life

Think of Drew's life and Chris, Jessie, Emily, and Logan. We can look back and say emphatically: They were not cheated by Drew's life with all the

157

challenges and difficulties that his health needs brought. They didn't draw the short straw. They weren't dealt a bad hand. They weren't shortchanged in any way.

They were blessed in a manner most are unaccustomed to and in a way that had much sacrifice attached to it. No one hundred-yard dash on those spindly little legs but there was a smile with oversized dimples that was every bit as rewarding and then some. No report card to hang on the fridge or post on social media but there was a laugh at the family's antics that melted hearts. That made the sacrifice more than worth it and taught an entire family how to love like nothing else could.

Heirs together of the gracious gift of life.
1 Peter 3:7 (NIV)

Drew's frailties made the appreciation of the gracious gift of life all the more real.

Not Cheated In Death

In the Gospel of Mark, there is the story of the paralyzed man being brought to Jesus by his friends. Jesus turned to the young man and said: "Son, your sins are forgiven."

What Jesus was giving had never been asked for, never verbalized. Jesus gave the man what his heart longed for even more than the healing of his body.

Chris and Jessie's heart for Drew always looked ahead to this time when Drew would experience freedom, wholeness in the presence of the Lord: Drew talking, walking, running, and jumping.

I am thankful for the times I was privileged to share about Jesus with Drew and to know that even though he couldn't answer me, he heard every word.

Maybe we can all take a lesson from his life about cherishing the gift of life—our own and those around us; about looking for those blessings in disguise; about knowing that no matter how great the challenge, our God is able to work all things for good and to make life the cherished treasure God intended.

You will receive a rich welcome into the eternal kingdom of our Lord and Savior Jesus Christ.
2 Peter 1:11 (NIV)

This might have been a memorial service of a young three-year-old child if the heart doctor's prediction had come to pass. Sixteen years have come and gone since that three-year estimate expired. This memorial service has become a celebration of life—the life of a blessing that far exceeded all expectations, wrapped up in the body of a young man with health issues of every scope and kind.

Cherish the gift of life that Andrew Parker Hall was to his family and loved ones.

We received great consolation from these words. One of the care workers read Drew one last story. We were thankful that we had the privilege of gathering together to say goodbye to our Angel Boy. Just a few days after the funeral, everything in Michigan shut down because of the pandemic, and God's faithfulness could be sensed in the timing of Drew's passing.

There have been three occasions where people saw Drew. One was a dream that a friend had. The other two were given to Drew's grandpa and to a pastor friend. They were like visions where they saw Drew all grown up. He was standing tall with reddish hair.

January 16 is Drew's birthday. He would have been twenty. Jessie arranged for a fleece blanket party where we tied together bright fabric prints. Many hands made 59 blankets. Some of the blankets were given to Drew's respite/hospice group. A second batch went to another hospice group in the area. This was such an uplifting way to honor Drew. We miss you, Drew.

WE ARE BECAUSE YOU WERE

Overshadowed by God's Sovereignty — Drew's Story

ACTS Prayer

Add your prayers here and meditate on the God who is sovereign over you. Have you come to the conclusion that His thoughts are far above your thoughts?

Adoration: I worship you as Sovereign God. You know what is best. You see a bigger picture than I do.

Confession: I repent for every time I doubted your plan, your love, your suffering for me, Jesus. Forgive me. I was ignorant of all that you suffered for me. I am sorry I didn't trust you, Lord.

Thanksgiving: Thank you for loving me when I was unlovable, when I was doubting, and when I was in sin. Thank you for bringing me through suffering. I didn't always know why, but you faithfully brought me through.

Supplication: I pray that you will bring everyone in my life to the saving knowledge of Jesus Christ. All the people in my life need You, Lord. Draw them close to You.

Overshadowed by God's Sovereignty — Drew's Story

Process What You Have Read

1. What circumstances have you experienced in your life where you didn't understand what was happening to you?

2. Did you think differently about God after that trial? Did you understand God's sovereignty?

3. How did you get through that time, or are you still dealing with the difficult situation?

4. Did you ever experience a blessing in disguise?

5. Have you had people come alongside of you through a trial?

6. Have you ever had a dream or a vision?

Overshadowed by God's Sovereignty — Drew's Story

Biblical Worldview on God's Sovereignty

◆ God shows His Sovereignty when He makes a covenant with Abraham.

◆ God shows His Sovereignty to Moses, Joshua, Gideon, Samson, David

◆ We can trust God in our circumstances when we know about God's sovereignty.

Trusting The Sovereign Lord In Our Circumstances — Psalm 71:5; Psalm 71:16; Psalm73:28; Psalm 109:21; Psalm 141:8; 1 Timothy 6:13-15; Revelation 6:10

> *God is to us a God of salvation; and to God the Lord*
> *belong ways of escape from death.*
> Psalm 68:20 (NASB)

The Lord's Covenant with Abraham — Genesis 15:1-5

Moses The Deliverer — Deuteronomy 3:23-24; 1 Kings 8:53

Joshua, Gideon, Samson — Judges 6:22; Judges 16:28; Joshua 7:7

David's Prayer — 2 Samuel 7:18-20; 2 Samuel 7:22; 2 Samuel 7:28-29

Chapter Eleven
Overshadowed in Everyday Life — Dianne's Bike Story

He who dwells in the secret place of the Most High shall
abide under the shadow of the Almighty.
Psalm 91:1 (NKJV)

Ahh! Time for a summer bike ride. The White Pine Trail is Michigan's second-longest biking trail. It follows the former Grand Rapids and Indiana train rail bed for 93.5 miles through five counties. My husband and I were biking north to Big Rapids from Stanton, Michigan. This is one of our favorite bicycle trails in Michigan. We were on one leg of the trail, and it wasn't long — about seven miles. In this section, people call it a "two-track," which is a grass and gravel path. To be honest, I didn't like the path we were on. A paved path is less effort as you peddle. Our plan was to bike out and back for a total of 14 miles — an easy ride. It was a gorgeous July day, but it was the hottest day we had experienced that month. The temperatures were in the 90's with high humidity.

I went for a swim before the bike ride, not knowing that this dip in the pool would be to my detriment. We didn't get an early start, so we were biking in the hottest part of the day. On our way back, I began to feel bad. I had a headache and felt like throwing up. I didn't want to quit riding. I kept going. (Let me remind the reader here that I'm married to a Marine.) A Marine wife can't quit! My competitive pride gets in the way from time to time. It's part of my flesh and it has to die!

We stopped for a rest, and Tony saw that my face was really flushed. I finished the last of my water. Tony took his bandana, soaked it with water from his bottle, and put it around my neck. The cool feeling refreshed me, and we continued biking. I went a mile or so. We stopped, and I said, "I've got to lie down." I knew this was a bad idea within myself, and as I plopped to the ground, it was another sign to

Tony that I was in bad shape. This wasn't normal behavior for me. Fourteen miles was not a big ride. What was my problem?

There I was on the ground. B-z-z-z, b-z-z-z. Horse flies started buzzing around my head. Ouch! One bit my hand. I decided that getting back on my bike and riding was better than getting more bites from the flies. Is it time to thank God for dreadful horseflies?

In everything give thanks; for this is the will of God in
Christ Jesus for you.
1 Thessalonians 5:18 (NKJV)

We began riding out of the trees and into the blazing sun again. One more mile, and we stopped for another drink from Tony's bottle. I was experiencing heat exhaustion. My time in the swimming pool before biking was the cause of my dehydration. Who knew?

We left the woods, and we were traveling on the dusty gravel road into the midday sun. There were fields on either side of the path planted with lush green crops of corn and beans. The blue-sky day was beautiful and boiling hot. Tony encouraged me: "It'll be better when we are in the shade." Large looming trees were in the distance with welcoming shade. As we reached these shady spots, I began to linger when we rode through the trees. The cool of the shade was comforting. Then, we rode out into the scorching sun again.

When my husband said, "It will be better in the shade," his words sparked my thinking. I remembered the shadow of the Most High in Psalm 91:1. I am living under God's shadow, God's shade. I began praying, "Help me, Lord. Give me strength to get through this ride." After a few more stops, we arrived at our truck. We had jugs of water in the truck, and I poured the cool water over my head. I was instantly refreshed. I thanked God I was able to finish the ride that day with God strengthening me. I thanked Him that my husband was with me, encouraging me all the way.

We try to do things in our own strength, and we need to realize that God's strength is more than enough. He is willing to strengthen us when we ask Him. You might think, "God isn't concerned about these insignificant occurrences in our lives." The truth is: God is concerned about us in the big and little circumstances of our lives...all things.

The Bible is filled with verses where God makes promises to those who belong to Him. If we don't know these promises, we cannot receive them. In the Secret Place of the Most High, I have heard God whisper: "Tell them I love them — tell them I care." That is why I write books, mentor women, encourage people, and pray for others. Telling people God loves them isn't difficult, and it's a truth we can count on. Jesus showed His love when He died for us on the cross.

Jesus loves you so very much! Jesus cares about you and everything that concerns you, big and little. Wherever Jesus walked on this earth, He took time to talk to people. He healed people. He loved people. He taught people about God the Father. He fed people. He showed us how much He loved us when He died on the cross and suffered all the punishment for our sins. Jesus warned us that we would have tribulation in our lives on this earth. He taught the people how to live. Do you try to do things in your own strength?

We see in the Bible how Moses, in the Old Testament, taught the people about God. Some people believed. Some died in the wilderness because of their unbelief. We see, in the New Testament, Jesus taught the people about the Father. Some people believed, and some did not believe. The people were free to choose. God gives us free will.

What do we see today? What is the same? When people hear the Gospel message, some believe, and others do not think so. What are you choosing? I choose to believe that I live overshadowed by the Most High!

Overshadowed in Everyday Life — Dianne's Bike Story

ACTS Prayer

Worship God as the Omnipresent One. Write out your own prayers in the spaces below.

Adoration: I worship you that you enable me to live under the shadow of the Almighty.

Confession: I confess to you, Lord, that I do not say the right things. I speak unbelief and doubt rather than what your Word says. So I speak your Word today: I will say of the Lord, "He is my refuge and my fortress; My God, in Him I will trust.

Thanksgiving: Thank you, Lord Jesus, for watching over me.

Supplication: I seek Your face, Lord, in the little things of life.

Overshadowed in Everyday Life — Dianne's Bike Story

Process What You Have Read

The Bike Story — is a short testimony written to show you that Jesus cares about everything in your life. He cares about where you go, who you are with, and what you do in your everyday life. Jesus said He would never leave us or forsake us. That means when you are bike riding or playing your favorite sport. He is right there with you. You can talk to Him as you peddle, ski, or hit a ball. You can pray as you ride on a bike, sit on a ski lift, or drive a golf cart.

1. Are you into sports? You know the thrill of getting outside! Which sports do you like?

2. When participating in your favorite sports, have you ever had injuries happen that you weren't expecting? Describe what took place.

3. Does God care about everything in our lives or just the "spiritual" things? Explain from your perspective.

4. Has it ever occurred to you that you could talk to God when you're enjoying sports? What examples can you give?

Overshadowed in Everyday Life — Dianne's Bike Story

Biblical Worldview of Standing By Faith

God Supplies And Equips Us With Spiritual Weapons
- ◆ Jesus Christ, the Lamb of God
- ◆ The Cross
- ◆ The Word of God
- ◆ The Blood of Jesus and Our Testimony
- ◆ The Armor of God
- ◆ The Name of Jesus
- ◆ The Holy Spirit
- ◆ The Second Coming of Jesus Christ

God has given us these provisions when we profess Jesus Christ as Lord and Savior.

Biblical References:

Jesus Christ, The Lamb of God — Revelation 7:17

Abraham said, "God will provide for himself the lamb for a burnt offering, my son." So they went both of them together.
Genesis 22:8 (ESV)

The next day he saw Jesus coming toward him, and said, "Behold, the Lamb of God, who takes away the sin of the world!"
John 1:29 (ESV)

"Let all the house of Israel therefore know for certain that God has made him both Lord and Christ, this Jesus whom you crucified."
Acts 2:36 (ESV)

The Cross — Galatians 6:14

> *For Christ did not send me to baptize but to preach the gospel, not with words of eloquent wisdom, lest the cross of Christ be emptied of its power.*
> 1 Corinthians 1:17 (ESV)

> *For the word of the cross is folly to those who are perishing, but to us who are being saved it is the power of God.*
> 1 Corinthians 1:18 (ESV)

The Word of God — 1 Corinthians 2:8

> *For the word of God is living and active, sharper than any two-edged sword, piercing to the division of soul and of spirit, of joints and of marrow, and discerning the thoughts and intentions of the heart.*
> Hebrews 4:12 (ESV)

The Blood of Jesus and Our Testimony

> *And they have conquered him by the blood of the Lamb and by the word of their testimony, for they loved not their lives even unto death.*
> Revelation 12:11(ESV)

The Armor of God

Belt of Truth, Breastplate of Righteousness, Shoes of Peace, Shield of Faith, Helmet of Salvation, Sword of the Spirit, and Prayer — Philippians 2:9-11

> *Finally, be strong in the Lord and in the strength of his might. Put on the whole armor of God, that you may be able to stand against the schemes of the devil. For we do not wrestle against flesh and blood, but against the rulers, against the authorities, against the cosmic powers over this present darkness, against the spiritual forces of evil in the heavenly places. Therefore take up the whole armor of God, that you may be able to withstand in the evil day, and having done all, to stand firm. Stand therefore, having fastened on the belt of truth, and*

having put on the breastplate of righteousness, and, as shoes for your feet, having put on the readiness given by the gospel of peace. In all circumstances take up the shield of faith, with which you can extinguish all the flaming darts of the evil one; and take the helmet of salvation, and the sword of the Spirit, which is the word of God, praying at all times in the Spirit, with all prayer and supplication. To that end, keep alert with all perseverance, making supplication for all the saints.
Ephesians 6:10-18 (ESV)

The Name of Jesus — John 16:23-24; John 14:13-14

And these signs will accompany those who believe: in my name they will cast out demons; they will speak in new tongues.
Mark 16:17(ESV)

The seventy-two returned with joy, saying, "Lord, even the demons are subject to us in your name!"
Luke 10:17 (ESV)

The Holy Spirit

But the Helper, the Holy Spirit, whom the Father will send in my name, he will teach you all things and bring to your remembrance all that I have said to you.
John 14:26 (ESV)

The Holy Spirit descended on him in bodily form, like a dove; and a voice came from heaven, "You are my beloved Son; with you I am well pleased."
Luke 3:22 (ESV)

The Second Coming of Jesus Christ

"Do not let your heart be troubled; believe in God,
believe also in Me. In My Father's house are many
rooms; if that were not so, I would have told you, because
I am going there to prepare a place for you. And if I go
and prepare a place for you, I am coming again and will
take you to Myself, so that where I am, there you also
will be. And you know the way where I am going."
John 14:1-4 (NKJV)

Jesus tells us that He's coming back for us, and He's preparing a place for us where we will be with Him forever. His promise is: He is coming to get His Bride. We are the Bride! Now that's Good News!

Chapter Twelve
Overshadowed by God's Presence — Evelyn's Story

Note from Evelyn to the reader:

"My hope is that the faithfulness and love of our precious Heavenly Father shines through this story. My testimony would be that in the darkest despairing time in my life when I cried out to the Lord, He heard me. From the depths of my heart in that hour, my agonizing cry was: 'God, you have to show Yourself in this. I am not going to make it if you don't show Yourself. It's too much. It's too much.' It has been many years since that horrific night and, yet, I can say He continues to answer that prayer."

Oh, the pain of loss! A loved one passes, and you feel it immediately — the ache in your heart, the difficulty breathing, and then the flood of thoughts. Time has just stood still — and your life is changed forever.

Nothing can settle you into the "now" more than death. Nothing can make you wish you could be anywhere else in time, and yet, here you are in today with your pain. For an instant, you question the sting. Then, you hear the exhortation, "Today, if you hear His voice, do not harden your heart." What will tomorrow hold? And all your tomorrows from this time forward?

The preacher says, "Life will get good again." You question that statement and cannot believe it.

Next, you read, "The God of all comfort will comfort you," and you wonder, "How can that be?"

The familiar Psalm 23 rings in your ear with new meaning: "Yea, though you walk through the valley of the shadow of death, you will fear no evil, for the Lord is with you." You take a breath, swallow the lump in your throat, and rest in His arms. Little did I realize the anguish that was yet to come.

173

I (Evelyn) lost my son Matt on December 16, 2004. He was twenty-six years old. I haven't a clue how anyone can endure the grieving process without trusting in God. The Bible says that Christians do not grieve as the world grieves — this is true...but we do grieve.

The following story is about my precious son Matt — gone from this life, but forever in my heart. Matt's story covers several seasons — the good, the bad, the ugly...and ultimately comfort and hope in the Lord.

Matt was born on July 28, 1978. He was the third of our six children. He loved the TV sitcom *Malcolm in the Middle*, and he was our Matthew in the middle. He was a unique joy to us and never gave us an ounce of trouble.

Beginning from the time Matt was a baby, he changed my life. He altered any career goals I had in my mind at that time. While I was on maternity leave from General Motors, Matt suffered from a respiratory condition that resulted in a collapsed lung and a lengthy hospital stay. Due to the economic crisis at that time, there was a season of cutbacks. My maternity leave was up, my baby was in the hospital, and I had two choices: return to work or resign. There was really only one decision that I felt compelled to make. So, I became a stay-at-home mom, and I am so thankful for that rare opportunity.

Matt was my cotton-topped, blue-eyed charmer. He was the child who would bring me dandelion bouquets, hug my knees, then be on his way to his next adventure. He was innocent and trusting, for he knew my kisses would heal his boo-boos. He held his heart in his hands, and just a smile would capture yours as well. When I met his kindergarten teacher for the first time, she shared a heartwarming story with me. Out of the blue, during the first week of school, Matt looked up at her with those big adoring blue eyes and said, "Mrs. T, you're beautiful." Mrs. T was a middle-aged teacher. She confided in me that no one had told her that in years. Needless to say, Matt won her heart that day. That's the kind

174

of boy Matt was. He saw beauty in the everyday things of life. He loved ice-covered trees in winter and the fragrance of lilacs in spring.

Matt's respiratory problems that developed during infancy decreased throughout his childhood. Although he was troubled with a couple of minor asthma attacks, this did not limit his physical activity. However, he was not an athletic child at all. His participation in sports rested solely on school requirements. Meanwhile, his two older brothers, only sixteen months apart, were inseparable. The two brothers were wrapped in their own world outside of Matt.

They were actively involved in sports and constantly competed with each other in everything, even in trivial matters, like eating breakfast quicker or finishing their chores faster.

Christian School Years

In first grade, Matt fell off a playground slide and broke his right hand. It was an extremely traumatic experience as I watched the ER doctor re-break the bone to set it in a cast. This was done without any anesthesia, and I can still see those painfully blue eyes looking up at me as I prayed over him. Despite this setback, Matt turned this trial into victory. With a cast on his right arm, he took the initiative to learn how to write with his left hand. With remarkable tenacity, his academics didn't miss a beat. He continued to maintain that ambidextrous skill throughout his years.

Exceptionally smart and self-motivated doesn't begin to describe my son. In first grade, his vocabulary ability was off the charts. He had proficiency in language like no one I knew. He was studious, conscientious, talented, and artistic. He was even self-taught in computer mastery.

With his command of the English language, there's no doubt Matt could have become an accomplished writer. He grew up watching the beloved TV series *The Waltons*. I could envision him as the modern-day Earl Hamner Jr., composing

175

stories of life in a large family. Matt was the John Boy of our household. Although I never had the pleasure to see his writing strength fully develop, I treasure Matt's writings that I do have.

Aside from Matt's academic achievements, he possessed endearing qualities that distinguished him from his peers. He was funny, loving, and sensitive. He was evangelical, a visionary, and most importantly, he was easily entreated by the Lord. After attending a Christian summer camp at the age of 11, he wrote,

> *"The Lord called me to the altar, having me not know what for, but to go in faith. He spoke to me while I was praying, for me to be a missionary. And while we were closing in a song, God gave me a Scripture to confirm it: 'But you shall receive power after the Holy Spirit has come upon you: and you shall be witnesses to me in Jerusalem, and in all Judea and Samaria, and to the ends of the earth.'*
> Acts 1:8 (NKJV)

> And also, a prophecy came forth concerning going out to the four corners of the earth. And that's my testimony."

That following Christmas season, Matt came home from the Christian school he attended and enthusiastically described an experience he had in the chapel that day. The guest speaker was a missionary from the Philippines who had challenged the students to go forth and preach the gospel. Matt answered the call, drew a nativity story picture, and proceeded to share the Christmas story with our next-door neighbors. My husband Bob and I were certain that this was only the beginning of a successful ministerial calling on our son's life.

Long after Matt's medical crisis, I returned to the workforce as a second income became essential to provide for the needs of our growing family. I worked a great deal, but I took advantage of working around the kids' schedules. I was able to take summers off to spend time with them. Over the course of the school year, I often worked afternoons, and my mother-in-law helped out considerably. She eased my workload by babysitting and assisting with household tasks. Matt was very close to his grandma as he had few friends. Although he struggled to connect with the other boys in the neighborhood, he did have a best friend right next door, little Michelle, who was the same age as Matt. She was the bright spot in his day, and her friendship provided him with the acceptance he so desperately wanted. They would sit in our backyard for hours under the big old cottonwood tree and share stories, hopes and dreams.

As he reached the turbulent adolescent years, the contrast between Matt and his peers became more evident. Out of jealousy, kids at school often teased his superior intellect. I sadly learned that the Christian school environment was far from ideal. To my dismay, bullying was not exempt within its "protective walls." Although he did have a couple of school friends, Matt would often be forced to endure the sneers and jeers of other classmates, as his scholarly aptitude set him apart from the pack. He was known as the kid whose "brain was on steroids." His vast attributes became a source of deep wounds for him. During the summer of eighth grade, Matt expressed his sadness by telling me, "Mom, nobody likes me. Do you know what it's like to have nobody like you?" That was the only indication of the struggles that he suffered.

My son felt rejected and was inconsolable. Although my heart went out to him, he was the least of our worries at the time. My husband and I were swamped with other teenage challenges as we scrambled to rein in our two older boys. We were constantly putting out fires created by their less than compliant mischief. Needless to say, we were overwhelmed and working on overload. Since Matt was a late bloomer in the area of typical teenage rebellion, we welcomed his honest dependability and trustworthiness. We were grateful for his capacity to remain low-maintenance and not require constant intervention. In hindsight, I see that we were so preoccupied with other levels of parenting we missed a lot of what Matt was going through. I have to say that as sensitive as he was, he hid his hurts well.

In Matt's senior year of high school, he fulfilled his childhood dream of going on the mission field. He accompanied a group of his classmates on a ten-day trip to the Philippines, and to say he was excited would be an understatement. While there, he spent his time performing drama skits on the streets and displaying the love of Jesus to the locals. His genuine concern for others and deep sensitivity touched the hearts of many.

I would love to say that Matt's mission trip ended on a good note. Unfortunately, it did not. Rejection from the other students followed him. On their way home, the group stopped in Hawaii for what was intended to be two tropical days of fun in the sun. But some of the kids decided to play a heartless prank by offering Matt what looked like a candy bar. In truth, it was an Ex-Lax chocolate bowel stimulant. Instead of spending his time on the beach with everyone else, he spent it alone in his hotel room. The previous excitement Matt had felt over this trip was overshadowed by dejection and misery. To add insult to injury, when my son arrived home, he was regretfully informed that his beloved Grandma had passed while he was away. He was heartbroken, and I don't think he ever quite recovered from the loss.

Yet, despite adversity, Matt pressed on and excelled, continuing his high standard of academic achievement. His senior year in high school was filled with honors and rewards for all his years of hard work. He received a certificate of merit from the National Merit Scholarship Program, was co-valedictorian of his class, and was awarded a full four-year scholarship complete with stipends from Lawrence Tech, a very exclusive, prestigious university where he was preparing to study architecture. Matt always put 110 percent into everything he endeavored to do, and we were so rightly proud of him. All things had fallen into place, and it appeared as though he was well on his way to success.

Valedictorian Speech

One of the most treasured of Matt's writings is his valedictorian speech. To briefly summarize, he began by expressing his appreciation to those who were instrumental in his life. He then directed his speech to his fellow students, encouraging them to achieve greatness and enter into all the wonderful things God had planned for them. There were also words of direction, stressing the importance of realizing precisely what to pursue, letting go of one's own plans, and allowing God's plan to take place. I find it amazing that Matt warned of pitfalls, stating that "it was harder to be a dedicated Christian in today's society than when the early church first began and suffered persecution." He spoke of "distractions and pressures to conform to the world's mixed-up standards." He powerfully stated that "we must be wary to not let the near-deafening messages they send drown out the still small voice of God in our hearts." He concluded by encouraging his peers "to go the extra mile, to discover their God-given potential and achieve it, to choose to do something, to dream something, to be pleasing to God because the decisions made now can determine the outcome of your life. Dare to dream."

Christians Do Not Have Insurance Policies Against Evil in This World

Such promise, such potential, such purpose in life. We knew our son was destined for great things, and then the flood came. It is incredibly difficult to reflect on, much less explain. I used to think that if I did all the right things, taught my children about the Lord, took them to church every time the doors were open, sacrificed to put them through Christian school, prayed for them earnestly, that I had an insurance policy—that everything was always going to be great in life. I believed that our family would never face some of the attacks or challenges that the world faces. Perhaps, I was still living on Walton's Mountain, and we were to live happily ever after. If I have learned anything over these past several years, it's that Christians do not have insurance policies against the evil in this world. Bad things do happen to good people. Hard times do come. (Consider our Old Testament friend Job) Yet, though we do not have an insurance policy, we do have a blessed assurance in the Lord.

Matt Reveals A Secret

So, buckle up as I take you on a roller coaster ride and provide a narrative of the next portion of my story. As arduous as it is to recount the events, I feel it is critical for those struggling with the pain of a prodigal son or daughter for whatever reason.

As wonderfully naïve as our former life was, it all came crashing down in one night — one confrontation which would alter our lives forever. Several months before that eventful night, I had observed that Matt's usual gregarious disposition was changing. I didn't know what the problem was, but he became distant, self-absorbed, stressed, and depressed. There was an apparent arrogance in him that I had never seen before. He avoided church attendance and was easily irritated with family life in general. I knew something was up but didn't know what. So, I did what I had learned to do over the years while raising teenagers — I began to pray that the Lord would reveal whatever was necessary. That can be a very unsettling prayer because if you pray it, be prepared for the Lord to be faithful to answer. It is said that the truth will set you free, but first, it will make you miserable. I can testify it goes beyond that. The truth I was about to receive made me more than miserable — it made me want to die.

On the now infamous date of December 16, 1997, ironically seven years to the day prior to Matt's death, my husband Bob and I were sitting in our dining room when Matt came in trembling and said that he needed to tell us something. "Mom and Dad, I'm gay."

Have you ever been caught in a tornado or a hurricane? I'm convinced that those five words carried a more devastating effect than any natural disaster is capable of. It was as though a bomb had exploded in our house.

That very night Matt moved out of our home, but never out of our hearts and prayers. We were on a different course From that day forward: uncharted, heartbreaking, and disastrous in its final analysis. Living in the mass media age that we are in, I had heard staggering statistics of the homosexual lifestyle. All of these came into focus that night.

I expressed my greatest fears to Matt while imploring: "Do you know that the road you are choosing is filled with promiscuity, drug abuse, sexually transmitted disease, not to mention HIV and AIDS? Life expectancy is half, and the suicide rate is triple that of heterosexuals!"

As I was pleading about these statistics, trying to reason with what was a totally unreasonable situation, Matt proved to be more naive than I. He was convinced that none of this was going to happen to him. Sadly, over the course of the next seven years, I suspect that most of it did happen. In desperation, I shoved his deceased grandmother's picture in his face and yelled: "You tell your Grandma!"

I dare say that as time went by, my son would be stunned at the bottomless pit one could spiral down into. As for me, the first few weeks were definitely the hardest. I was overwhelmed by the initial news and the myriad of emotions attached to it. Paralyzed in my own pain, I couldn't even leave my bedroom, sequestered alone in my solitude. It's been said that when our kids come out of the closet, the parents go in. I became a recluse while I cried and cried and cried some more. I pleaded with God. I couldn't eat. Death seemed sweeter.

Eventually, and out of necessity, my first venture out of my bedroom was to go to the grocery store, where I literally had to pray my way down every aisle. I did what I had to do and then came home and retreated back to my room, where I felt safe.

Bob and I were careful about disclosing our plight. We kept it mainly to ourselves and discreetly revealed it to only those closest to us. Well-meaning friends reached out in an attempt to console me, yet not understanding what I was going through. It was a scenario that none of my immediate peer group could identify with. They could sympathize, but they could not empathize. We carried such an acute sense of shame and failure. I never felt so alone in my life.

I had millions of questions. How does this happen? What did I do wrong? What did I miss in Matt's formative years? What could I have done differently? Surely, this was my fault—after all, moms seem to bear the blame for what happens in our children's lives. My life became filled with tears, prayers, questions, and sadness. In the midst of my despair, I learned of a new beatitude: Blessed are the desperate, for they shall find hope in God.

On the first Sunday that I felt emotionally capable of returning to church, I made it into the back door, through the kitchen, and to the back row of the sanctuary. From there, I went through the nursery and into the pastor's office, where Bob and I spent the next two hours crying, with the assistant pastor attempting to console us. The word that he gave us, which I continue to hold onto even today, is: "Hope thou in God."

Sad Life

I wish I could interject some beautiful passage here, but it was neither a beautiful nor gay time. There was nothing gay about Matt's lifestyle. Someone has aptly suggested that it should be called "sad" for truly Matt lead a sad life. Initially, over the course of the first few months, I had a desperate desire to fix my son. I have since learned that this is a common thread among parents in similar situations. Looking for that new or perhaps old insurance policy…where was it now?

Barbara Johnson's Story

There have been many ironies on my journey. One is exposure to author Barbara Johnson's highly acclaimed book *Where Does a Mother Go to Resign?* A friend had given me her book many years earlier simply because she was so impressed with the author's testimony.

For those unfamiliar with her story, I will briefly summarize: Barbara had four sons. Two died five years apart, one in Vietnam, the other at the hands of a drunk driver. Then the bomb fell with her third son proclaiming his homosexuality. In her memoir, one scene that stood out to me more than anything was the comment she made to her son in the heat of an argument — we parents are capable of saying anything out of desperation. Her comment was: "I'd rather you be dead than gay." Continuing her story, she recounts how her son changed his name, disowned his family, and was estranged from them for eleven years. Being acutely aware of this possibility, I became very cautious of the way I communicated with Matt. Beyond anything else, my greatest fear was that he would walk out of our lives, and I wouldn't know where he was or how he was faring. He moved out of our home and into the home of a much older man who was his boyfriend and mentor. Less than ten days later, Matt spent his first Christmas alone while his boyfriend attended his own family holiday function without him. It was evident that our son still needed us in his life.

Loving Unconditionally And Trusting God

Gradually, we started processing this new walk we were on. We began rebuilding our shattered relationship, agreeing to disagree and love one another despite our differences. I slowly realized that I couldn't fix my son, that I could only love him unconditionally, which I did with my whole heart. I had to trust God to fix him how He saw fit. By the same token, Matt unhappily and reluctantly accepted the fact that although we loved him dearly, we continued to disapprove of what he was doing. At one point, Matt wanted a commitment service with his boyfriend, but I just couldn't be a part of that. As much as I loved him and wanted to get along, I simply could not betray my core being.

Assurance Policy

In her book, *Where Does a Mother Go to Resign*, Barbara Johnson uncovers what so many of us parents experience. She endured depression, therapy, and hopelessness. She described it as being "in a black box with no light, only darkness, and void." Her little ray of light came in the form of a note I'm about to share and was also a ray of hope for me and an answer to my assurance policy.

Barbara's first question: "Can a twenty-year-old Christian young person be hooked into homosexuality?"

And this was the pastor's response: "Absolutely! A Christian can get hooked into sin."

Yes, a twenty-year-old can fall into fornication.

Adultery, yes.

Drugs, yes.

Christians may be tempted and fall into sin even after they become Christians.

One can fall into all kinds of evil.

The magnificence of Christianity is that Jesus Christ will not let you stay there. He won't let you stay there, and I'll tell you why.

One, you are His property! You are not your own. You were purchased with a price: the blood of the cross. If you think you are going to become a Christian, fall into some sin, stay in it and be happy, then you should think again — because you're miserable. And not only that, if you persist in the sin, He might destroy your physical body in order that your spirit will be saved."

184

*"Deliver such a one to Satan for the destruction of the
flesh, that His spirit may be saved in the day of the Lord
Jesus."*
1 Corinthians 5:5 (NKJV)

Barbara's second question was: "Can we hope for his return
to God?"

The pastor's response was: "If the child belongs to God,
either God will bring him to repentance and healing or God
will judge. But one thing you can count on, if the child really
has been the Lord's, the Lord is going to give special attention
to that child! The Lord never gives up on His children. God
always looks for the prodigal. Yes, you can hope for the Lord
to touch that boy. Leave him in the hands of Christ and pray
for him."

It's one thing to read this on the pages of an inspiring book;
quite another to walk it out in your own life. Yet, that's what I
began to do.

Where Was God In All Of This?

Where was God in all of this? He was there in my quiet
times, in my desperate hours. He was there when I languished
before Him, still hoping against hope to repair Matt. He was
there when I was on my face before Him, agonizing, grieving,
and yet, always hoping. With His presence came the
awareness that this wouldn't be a short trial and there
wouldn't be a quick fix. But there was an assurance that this
indeed would pass, as all trials do. By God's unfailing grace,
He did not give me the foresight to know its conclusion.

I attend a support group from time to time for parents of
LGTBQ children called Healing Hearts. We meet together to
voice our brokenness in a non-judgmental, understanding
environment. Frequently, we are visited by newly aware
parents who are still in the "fix-it" stage of their private
distress. I continue to attend on occasion with one goal in
mind--and it's the same encouragement that I will give you,

the reader: Love your kids, accept them, and leave the rest to God.

Matt's seven-year ordeal was fraught with turbulence and misery. The dysfunctional on-again, off-again liaison with his older boyfriend, was often highly volatile. Once, I accidentally received a pocket call from Matt's phone. (He had no idea I was on the other end.) He and his boyfriend were in the middle of an explosive argument that could have easily escalated into violence. At that moment, I realized my helplessness and did the only thing I knew to do — pray.

One year before his death, Matt attempted suicide with an overdose of pills and alcohol. Before he could follow through, he was mercifully found and taken to the hospital, where he spent one week in ICU. Throughout that entire episode, I held on to a shred of hope that this would be a turning point in my son's life. Unfortunately, I was mistaken. The painful cycle continued to unfold.

Dreaded Diagnosis

In April 2004, Matt was diagnosed with fungal meningitis. More tests ensued which led us to even worse news: Matt was HIV-positive. I was with my son in the hospital room when the doctor told him the devastating report. We were shell-shocked. How could things get any worse? In stunned response, Matt looked at me and said, "I guess you were right, Mom." But I didn't want to be right! Please, God, tell me I am wrong! Then, without thinking and completely led by the Holy Spirit, I replied to my terrified son, "If I was right about that, could I have been right about Jesus loving you more than I do?"

Heart-Wrenching Mystery

The HIV diagnosis changed Matt forever. He was never the same after that. I was willing to dig my heels in and take care of him if and when the disease progressed, but he continued the turbulent relationship with his partner, and I remained at a distance, loving him the only way I knew how.

Matt's life ended tragically on December 16, 2004. On that day, as I knew it, my world ceased to exist, and the pain of losing him remains inconceivable. I must say that his death was shrouded with confusion and mystery. To this day, there are still unanswered questions. The events surrounding that devastating night started with a phone call from the Detroit Police Department around 7:00 PM. After verifying our parentage, the officer instructed us to call an inner-city hospital an hour away. No other details were disclosed at that time, and so the nightmare and panic began. Bob and I raced to the hospital alone on that cold, snowy night to face the most indescribably painful event of our lives. Because the hospital had listed Matt as "John Doe," it seemed like an eternity before we were able to see him. Eventually, we spotted Matt's boyfriend in the hallway, and he collapsed on the floor crying: "Didn't they tell you?" When we finally did see our son, it was through a glass door. He was already gone. He was lying on a cold slab with a white sheet covering him up to his mid-chest. There were no visible scrapes or bruises on his upper body. In that one dreadful moment, we were forced to acknowledge the most heart-wrenching reality: our sweet, beautiful son had left us.

Matt's cause of death was labeled "indeterminate." He was found lying in the street with his back broken. The coroner concluded that his injuries were not conducive to jumping but rather to being hit by a car. However, Matt's boyfriend presented us with a suicide note after his death, presumably written by Matt. The police called it a "cold case with no witnesses." Was it suicide? Possibly. Was he the victim of a hit-and-run driver? This is also a possibility. Sometimes, I wish I had the money to begin a full-out investigation. I've inquired of the Lord many times with no answers forthcoming.

While I can relive each moment of that fateful night, it is still almost too painful to put into words. The only expression

I can share was the agonizing cry that came from the depths of my soul—screams of unbelief of what my eyes behold as true. With every ounce of my being, I cried, "God, I have got to see You in this! You have got to show Yourself in this! This is too much! I'm not going to make it if You don't reveal Yourself!"

After hours of hysteria, phone calls, and exhausted sleep, I awoke the next morning to realize that this nightmare was indeed real. Oh, how I wished it had only been a horrible dream! But it was reality, and my son was gone. How were we ever going to get through this? So, the questions began, and to this day, there are still too many unanswered.

I had lost loved ones in the past, but this grief I was facing was not only tremendous anguish. It was also mixed with feelings of guilt, blame, and confusion. When death is partnered with tragedy, it can shake one's faith to the very foundation. After all these years, I'm still searching, still questioning, still reluctantly accepting what is humanly unacceptable.

Teach Me To Live The Impossible

A parent should never have to plan their child's funeral. Yet, Bob and I found ourselves with that very task. When I begged God to show himself, He did—in an outpouring of love from the body of believers. Close friends even helped me with the daunting burden of making funeral arrangements. The funeral home was packed to capacity, resulting in standing-room-only. The Lord enabled me to speak at my son's funeral. These are the words He put on my heart:

> "There is a story starting in Genesis of a man
> named Abraham; he was a man that believed
> God. Of the many events that are recorded in the
> Bible of Abraham's life, there is one that I have
> struggled with for many years. My Bible titles
> the chapter as "The Offering of Isaac." In a
> seeming test of Abraham's trust in God, the Lord
> asked him to blindly (that is in blind faith) offer

188

up his beloved son Isaac as a sacrifice to the Lord. Isaac was the son of promise, the son of his old age, the son that was to usher in many generations.

I have read this story many times over the years and could never understand why the Lord would test him in such away. I would relate this story to my own children and say: "Lord, I just don't know that I could do that." I don't understand that level of trust or faith, and I certainly didn't have it."

Periodically, the Lord would touch my heart with this story, and I would respond in a myriad of ways, none being that of "acceptance." I would argue or go into denial and share with the Lord I didn't want to discuss it: "Could we just take this chapter out of the Bible?" Having been orphaned at a young age, I have been acquainted with grief but, the thought of losing a child (at any age) has been more than I could fathom.

Let me shift here for a few moments from Abraham's story to the here and now and share my heart about being a parent.

James Dobson once said that parenting isn't for cowards. I didn't know just how much courage and strength it would take at times.

Having raised four sons and going around the last lap with my last two children, needless to say, we've gone through some things.

It is also said: as parents, we give our children roots, and then we give them wings. I never understood until this week that only God can help them fly. Hopefully, along the way, you learn some things: you learn to laugh, you learn to cry, you learn to pray, you learn to say "I'm sorry," and most importantly, you learn to hug them frequently and tell them you love them. Having done all that, you stand on God's promises. You become more of a spectator in their lives with an occasional opportunity to continue to speak into their lives and pray and pray and pray.

I've prayed a lot for Matt in the past few years. We didn't always see eye to eye, but we always saw heart to heart.

I didn't like the road we were on any more than I like the story of offering Isaac, but I can say through it all, the Lord has been enlarging my faith and my love for my children.

Several months ago, I went to a ladies' conference, and the message of the weekend was of all things: "Lay your Isaac down." Once again, my soul travailed for my son Matt. Once again, I wrestled with the Lord, but I was beginning to see that only safe place for Matt was in his Heavenly Father's care. So, once more, I responded to the altar call and surrendered Matt to the Lord. I did not know that before the year ended, he would take him home.

In all of this, if I glean anything, I see more clearly the heart of God. "For God so loved the world that He gave His only begotten son so that whosoever believe in Him would not perish but have everlasting life." God did what no human parent can do because He loves us all. It's another mystery that we can't quite comprehend. This I know: God is good; God is love; God is faithful, and I praise Him that He is ever-present. I wouldn't be here today if that weren't so.

And so, with sadness, and yet with joy, today
I lay my Isaac down for the last time and share
the words to a precious song I heard that life-
changing special weekend. It is simply called
Isaac."

The flood of concern and support from so many touched
Bob and me on a very personal level. Two things have been
too numerous to count: one is tears, and the other is prayers.
Gradually my prayers have changed from: "God show
Yourself in this!" to "HELP!" and "Teach me to live the
impossible." Slowly, surely, daily, He is doing that. One of the
ways He has done that is by using other people to comfort me
and walk alongside me in this process.

Along with all of the positive feedback from so many, we
received a very wise piece of counsel from our pastor while we
were preparing for Matt's public viewing. He cautioned us
that sometimes people say stupid things. I'm so glad that he
warned us as it held much truth.

"It's not that people intend to say mean things; it's just that
they don't know what to say," he told us.

And really, beyond an "I'm sorry," what else can be said?

As so many would ask, "How are you doing?"

I came up with a pat answer: "On a scale from 1 to 10, I'm
about a minus zillion."

Fast forward a couple of weeks, and the stupidest thing
throughout this whole experience came from someone who
commented: "I thought that you would be in the positive
numbers by now."

It's been many years since, and I still keep a little paragraph
in my Bible as a reminder of the grieving process. It says:

"The reality is that you will grieve forever. You
will not "get over" the loss of your loved one.
You will learn to live with it. You will heal, and
you will rebuild yourself around the loss you
have suffered. You will be whole again, but you

191

will never be the same. Nor should you be the same. Nor would you want to be."

How Will This Affect Our Marriage

Some may ask how my son's death affected my marriage. I was fully aware of the statistics that most couples break apart after a child's death. I consciously purposed not to let that happen. Bob and I participated in a six-week marriage enrichment course through our church. The most profound piece of inspiration I gleaned was surprisingly in the book of Revelation, where Jesus proclaims that He holds the keys to hell and death. Our Lord is triumphant! I knew Bob and I were walking together with our Lord. The day will come when He will wipe away our tears, and there will be no more suffering. As a couple, we choose to hold on to hope.

There have been lessons to learn, and I continue to learn those lessons. Lessons such as loving unconditionally and walking in forgiveness. I understood I had forgiveness issues and had a wound that needed to be healed. As I searched my heart, I realized I needed to forgive Matt for being gay. And what about those people in my son's life that contributed to his demise? What about those he companioned with that led to the crash course that ended his life so prematurely? How about his mentor, who "showed him the ropes?" How was I to face that wound?

Pain Upon Pain, Forgiveness Upon Forgiveness

Facing it came sooner than I was prepared for as Matt's boyfriend showed up for the funeral. Exactly how much pain can a mother bear at once? Nevertheless, love and forgiveness found their place among our grief, as we welcomed him to sit at our table during the dinner afterward. I learned that it was imperative that I keep my wound clean — such wise council; such a hard lesson to learn and endure. Yet, over time, I've come to the conclusion that if my son's life is to matter and count, I must live a life of love and forgiveness.

Over the course of years preceding Matt's death, I had learned to love him unconditionally, regardless of his destructive choices over which I had no control. Now, I had to learn to forgive and face the consequences of how those choices would affect my family and me. Truly, no man is an island; none of us live or die to ourselves. There is a powerful message to be spoken about forgiveness, and it is best summed up in the Book of Ephesians:

> Let all bitterness, wrath, anger, clamor, and evil
> speaking, be put away from you, with all malice. And be
> ye kind one to another, tenderhearted, forgiving one
> another, even as God in Christ forgave you.
> Ephesians 4:31-32 (NKJV)

The road to forgiveness is often lonely and seemingly unfair. It is truly the road less traveled. However, I knew that if I harbored unforgiveness, I would stop up my well — the well that Jesus says will flow like living waters in those who believe.

Matt's favorite Christian song's lyrics were *Draw Me Close to You, Never Let Me Go.* That became my continual prayer for him through those turbulent years — that the Lord would never ever let him go. Secondly, Matt had a special Scripture that he shared in his senior year, and we had it inscribed on his tombstone:

> We have this treasure in earthen vessels, that the
> excellence of the power may be of God and not of us.
> 2 Corinthians 4:7 (NKJV)

When I consider Matt's struggles, I think about Samson in the Old Testament. In a few brief verses, we learn of Samson's moral decline and bad choices that he consequentially paid the price for. Samson was stripped of God's power at the end of his life, blinded, and destined to spend his remaining years in a dungeon. At his lowest point, Samson pleaded with the Lord, and the Lord heard his cry. I believe God has remembered my son Matt as well.

Matt's death will continue to remind me to love unconditionally and to walk in forgiveness — to always nurture faith, hope, and love. When I look out into the world these days, I see many hurting people in need of comfort. I can truly say that I have experienced the God of all comfort, and He is more than enough. I also see broken vessels like Matt, who have no answers of their own. They need prayer, and they need love. My prayer is:

"Lord, help me to be a vessel of mercy. Continue to bind up the brokenhearted and comfort all who mourn, as only You can do. Deposit a seed of hope in every desperate heart."

Hold On To Hope

I believe there are some reading this who are going through very hard times right now. I'm not talking about the normal rough and tough trials of life, but the ones that try to seize your faith and try to steal, kill, and destroy you. The times that cause you to gasp for breath and make you wonder how and why your heart is still beating. Those times are often referred to as "the dark night of the soul." I'm here to encourage you to hold on to hope because there is a light at the end of the tunnel for you.

For those whose life happens to be great at this moment, perhaps there is a nugget or two you can put in your pocket for a rainy day.

I have shared Matt's story in a panoramic view: the blissfully good years filled with joy and blessings and the fatally disastrous bad and ugly years that preceded his death. It's been many years since that fateful night that changed all our lives forever, and yet, the pilgrimage continues. I am reminded of some profound words that a dear friend of mine said back then: "Mary, you never get over this; it just gets different." And so it has.

It's so easy to compartmentalize my journey. With Matt, I could speak of the first nineteen years of his life that were so good, so blessed. Then, there are the last seven years that speak of struggle and bondage, and torment. A time when I witnessed my fears coming to pass even though I earnestly travailed in prayer for this precious child of mine. His death remains an enigma to this day and, yet, by faith, I stand on the promise of his eternity being spent with the Lord. Though he is gone, he does still speak, and that is what I wish to convey.

What do you do when life doesn't make sense? When God's promises seem to fail? When His Word appears to be contradicting itself? When you know in your heart, these things can't be true, and yet in your spirit, you try to make sense of it all?

- God's Word says that we see through a glass dimly, and yes, these past several years have been dim. What have I gleaned from these years, if ever so dimly? Life goes on even if you don't want it to. Babies are born, other loved ones pass away, employment comes and goes, life goes on and on and on.
- I've also learned that God's promises are true. He is faithful and His ways are perfect.
- My confusion has been replaced with a further revelation of His Word.

I continue on this journey, holding on to the Lord, or more accurately, I would say He holds on to me. Only by His amazing grace and love have I made it this far. I'm trusting Him to see me through to the finish line.

How will our story end? How long will it last? Will we survive it all? These are some of the questions I had at the beginning of my encounter as a parent of a wayward child. At that time, I hadn't a clue what I was about to face. But I can answer a few of those questions now. The tale unfolded tragically with the death of my son. Though that particular piece of the story ended after seven years of heartache and sorrow, the journey continues on a different path.

I remember stories that my young children used to read. There were several endings, and you could pick the one you liked best. In my humanness, I would like to have picked a different ending to our story, but life isn't like that after all. I'm sure that every parent who experiences the heartache of a wayward child desires to see them healed, whole, happy, and serving and loving the Lord with all their hearts. Though we can't choose the ending, we can choose some of the roads we take in its process.

Words Of Encouragement

With hindsight, all I can offer to parents are these words of encouragement:

- Love your children and help them to know that they are loved.
- You can stand your ground on what you believe is right and true, and it's important that you do so, for that is the core of your being. But in doing so, always remember that sin is sin, and there is only one cure for that — the precious Blood of Jesus. In the area of sin, may the Lord help us all?
- Through this journey, I have become aware that I am stronger than I ever knew I could be.
- Also, I've been weaker than I ever hoped to admit.
- I've been confronted with moments of helplessness, hopelessness, anguish, and despair. Ultimately, I've learned to lean on the Lord like never before.
- In so doing, I've received His comfort, His peace, a new assurance of faith, and the glorious, wonderful awareness of His Presence always.

That would be my prayer for everyone reading this, for there is no safer or better place to be than…in…His…Presence.

Gladness And Joy

I'm not sure exactly when, after Matt's death, God began to minister gladness to me, but He has even shown me joy again. At first, I'm sure it was a thimble at a time. The grief was so unbearable that I would have to remind myself to breathe. At other times, I would have been just as happy not to ever to breathe again.

Life is often a grueling quest. As we walk the path, we learn to accept the new "normal" in our lives, though totally perplexed, questioning, and unable to understand it all. We slowly learn to trust God. Life does get good again, as unbelievable as it seems in the beginning.

Scripture says that "weeping may endure for the night," and I've found that to be so. Weeping can endure, and endure, and endure, sometimes for a very long night. However, joy does come in the morning. Beyond today and tomorrow and possibly the next few years, Lord willing, you'll hear a voice whisper: "Comfort ye, comfort ye my people wherewith the same comfort you have been comforted." You have experienced Him like never before. You have wept together with no words spoken. You are of one heart. He loves you. He feels your pain. Then, somewhere in this thing, we call time, a miracle happens. Your pain is replaced with joy, for then, you gain a glimpse of the portals of heaven, and your tears are wiped away...by God Himself. Amen.

In the midst of the deepest sorrow, God overshadows His people with His Presence.

> *And the Lord replied, "I myself will go with you and give you success." For Moses had said, "If you aren't going with us, don't let us move a step from this place.*
> Exodus 33:14-15 (TLB)

> *You will show me the path of life; In Your presence is fullness of joy; At Your right hand are pleasures forevermore.*
> Psalm 16:11 (NKJV)

For I am not ashamed of the gospel of Christ, for it is the power Of God to salvation for everyone who believes, for the Jew first And also for the Greek.
Romans 1:16 (NKJV)

Overshadowed by God's Presence — Evelyn's Testimony

ACTS Prayer

Worship the Lord as His Presence surrounds you. Write your prayers in the spaces.

Adoration: I worship you, Father, on this, the worst day of my life. Give me your Presence. I need joy in your Presence. I need your eternal pleasures.

Confession: I confess that I was angry at You, God. I blamed you for what happened. I confess my sin and ask you to forgive me.

Thanksgiving: Thank you for giving me the truth from your Word as I look to you for answers.

Supplication: I pray that you will keep us from evil and that we will be close to your Presence. Overshadow us, Lord. We cry out to you today.

Overshadowed by God's Presence — Evelyn's Testimony

Process What You Have Learned

1. What surprised you in Evelyn's Testimony?

2. Do you have any LGTBQ people in your life? Explain.

3. Did you think that as a Christian, you have an insurance policy against evil?

4. What do you see in Mary's life that you would call resilient?

5. What makes you resilient in the hard times that you have experienced?

6. Have you ever felt that the Lord had forsaken you? When?

Overshadowed by God's Presence — Evelyn's Testimony

Biblical Worldview on Homosexuality

◆ The world says the Bible doesn't say anything about homosexuality. That's not true. The Bible has many things to say about homosexuality.

◆ God says that homosexuality is a sin. (God's word for it)

◆ We have hope — God made provision for sin. Jesus Christ, God's Son, died for our sins. God forgives sin because Jesus is the atoning sacrifice given for all men.

Biblical References:

What Does the Bible Say — Genesis 1:31; Matthew 19:4-5; Genesis 9:7; 1 Corinthians 6:9-10

> *So God created man in his own image; in the image of God he created him; male and female He created them.*
> Genesis 1:27 (NKJV)

> *For this reason God gave them up to vile passions. For even their women exchanged the natural use for what is against nature. Likewise also the men, leaving the natural use of the woman, burned in their lust for one another, men with men committing what is shameful, and receiving in themselves the penalty of their error which was due.*
> Romans 1:26-27 (NKJV)

God Calls It Sin — (God's Word For It) — Leviticus 20:13; 1Corinthians 6:9-11; Psalm 51:4; 1 Timothy 1:8-10

> *You shall not lie with a male as with a woman. It is an abomination.*
> Leviticus 18:22 (NKJV)

As Sodom and Gomorrah, and the cities around them in a similar manner to these, having given themselves over to sexual immorality and gone after strange flesh, are set forth as an example, suffering the vengeance of eternal fire.
Jude 1:7 (NKJV)

We Have Hope Because God Provides A Way Out Of Sin —
Jesus Christ — Romans 6:23; Romans 10:9; Romans 10:12-13; Romans 12:1-2; Isaiah 64:6; 1 Corinthians 6:18-20; John 3:16

For all have sinned and fall short of the glory of God.
Romans 3:23 (NASB)

But God demonstrates his own love toward us, in that while we were still sinners, Christ died for us.
Romans 5:8 (NASB)

If we say that we have no sin, we are deceiving ourselves and the truth is not in us. If we confess our sins, He is faithful and righteous, so that He will forgive us our sins and cleanse us from all unrighteousness. If we say that we have not sinned, we make Him a liar and His word is not in us.
1 John 1:8-10 (NASB)

Book Summary

We see a common thread in every testimony presented on these pages — when the people believed that God was real, believed God loves them, when they knew they could trust God with their lives, they began to flourish. God sewed gold threads of hope in the fabric of every story. He has gold strands of hope to embellish your life.

Another common thread in each testimony is the forward movement each person took. We have to forget our failures, faults, disappointments, sins and walk into our future. We cannot walk forward if we are looking back.

> *But one thing I do: forgetting what is behind and straining toward what is ahead, I press on toward the goal to win the prize for which God has called me heavenward in Christ Jesus. [Following Paul's Example] All of us, then, who are mature should take such a view of things. And if on some point you think differently, that too God will make clear to you.*
> Philippians 3:13-15 (NIV)

There is power in the Gospel of Jesus Christ. There is power in a person's testimony of God's salvation. Transformed lives are the result of hearing the truth. The truth sets people free. The Bible teaches: Everyone is invited to come into the Kingdom of God.

> *For I am not ashamed of this Good News about Christ. It is God's powerful method of bringing all who believe it to heaven. This message was preached first to the Jews alone, but now everyone is invited to come to God in this same way.*
> Romans 1:16 (TLB)

God invited Tony, Dianne, Laura, Rose, Zechariah, Elizabeth, Mary, Joseph, Christie, Steve, Beth, Corrie ten Boom, Chris, Jessie, Drew, Evelyn, and Matthew into the Kingdom. The same invitation is there for you. Jesus loves you! We have seen the overshadowing of the Most High in the lives of ordinary people. Your story comes on the next page. You are the next chapter.

Walk it forward, saint of God; your destiny begins now as you follow Jesus!

Personal Testimony Page

This page is reserved for you to write your testimony of God's goodness in your life.

How did God get your attention? How has God overshadowed you? When? Where?

Title your story by using these words:

OVERSHADOWED by _____

Appendix One — All About Testimony

(To be used with Chapter One)

All About Testimony — Isaiah 8:16; 1 John 5:10-12; Matthew 15:19; Matthew 27:13; Mark 14:57; Deuteronomy 5:20l; Psalm 78:56; John 5:31-32; Acts 2:40; John 2:25

> *This is the One who came by water and blood, Jesus Christ; not with the water only, but with the water and with the blood. It is the Spirit who testifies, because the Spirit is the truth. For there are three that testify: the Spirit and the water and the blood; and the three are in agreement. If we receive the testimony of people, the testimony of God is greater; for the testimony of God is this, that He has testified concerning His Son.*
> 1 John 5:6-9 (NASB)

John the Baptist Testifies About Jesus

> *The next day he saw Jesus coming to him, and said, "Behold, the Lamb of God who takes away the sin of the world!*
> John 1:29 (NASB)

> *And John testified, saying, "I have seen the Spirit descending as a dove out of heaven, and He remained upon Him.*
> John 1:32 (NASB)

The Ark of the Covenant is called — The Ark of the Testimony — 1 Samuel 6:19

> *When the Ark is finished, place inside it the stone tablets inscribed with the terms of the covenant, which I will give to you.*
> Exodus 25:16 (NLT)

Appendix Two

(To be used with Chapter Two — additional song lyrics)

The Story Behind "It Is Well With My Soul" and the Lyrics for the Song

This incredible story of faith belongs to Horatio Spafford (1828-1888). Much like Job, he placed his trust in God during his life's prosperity and also during life's calamities. A devout Christian who had immersed himself in Scripture, many years of his life were joyous. He was a prominent Chicago lawyer, whose business was thriving. He owned several properties throughout the city. He and his beloved wife had four beautiful daughters and one son. Life was more than good; it was blessed.

But faith, no matter how great, does not spare us from adversity. Just as Horatio hit the pinnacle of his profession and financial success, things began to change. It began with the tragic loss of their son. When Horatio Jr. was four years old, he died of scarlet fever.

In October 1871, dry weather and an abundance of wooden buildings, streets, and sidewalks made Chicago vulnerable to fire. The Great Chicago Fire began on the night of October 8, in or around a barn located on the property of Patrick and Catherine O'Leary at 137 DeKoven Street on the city's southwest side. Legend holds that the blaze started when the family's cow knocked over a lighted lantern; however, Catherine O'Leary denied this charge, and the true cause of the fire was never determined. What is known is that the fire quickly grew out of control and moved rapidly north and east toward the city center. The fire burned from October 8 to October 10, 1871, destroyed thousands of buildings, killed an estimated 300 people and caused an estimated $200 million in damages.[17] The Great Chicago Fire destroyed nearly every real estate investment Horatio Spafford owned.

Just a few years later, in 1873, Horatio decided to treat his wife, Anna, and daughters to a much-needed escape from the turmoil of life. He sent them on a boat trip to Europe, with plans to join them shortly after wrapping up some business in Chicago. The Spafford daughters were Annie, Maggie, Bessie, and Tanetta. They drowned when the *S.S. Ville du Havre* sank after it was hit by a British vessel en route to Europe in November 1873. A fellow survivor of the collision, Pastor Weiss, recalled Anna saying, "God gave me four daughters."

A few days later, Horatio received a heartrending telegram from his wife, Saved, but saved alone. What shall I do? It bore the excruciating news that the family's ship had wrecked and all four of his daughters had perished.

The rescue ship Tremountain took the survivors to Cardiff. During this voyage, Anna said few words. A friend who had also survived the sinking, clergymen Thoeophile Lorriaux, was with her when she finally uttered the words: "God gave me four daughters. They have been taken. One day I shall understand why. I will understand why."***

Inspiration and Solace: the Hymn

"Horatio left Chicago to meet Anna, who was staying with friends in France. At one point during the voyage, the ship's captain summoned Horatio to his cabin and explained that he had determined the exact spot where the *Ville du Havre* had gone down. He let Horatio know that they were at that moment passing that very spot. Horatio then returned to his own cabin, and, leaning for strength on his tremendous faith in God, wrote his famous hymn."[18]

Horatio was on his way to meet his heartbroken Anna, passing over the same sea that had just claimed the lives of his remaining children. It was then that he put his pen to paper, and the timeless hymn was born, beginning with the words:

208

When peace like a river attendeth my way
When sorrows like sea billows roll
Whatever my lot, Thou hast taught me to say
It is well, it is well with my soul

Refrain: It is well (it is well)
With my soul (with my soul)
It is well, it is well with my soul

Though Satan should buffet, though trials should come
Let this blest assurance control
That Christ has regarded my helpless estate
And has shed His own blood for my soul

Refrain: It is well (it is well)
With my soul (with my soul)
It is well, it is well with my soul

My sin, oh the bliss of this glorious thought
My sin, not in part, but the whole
Is nailed to the cross, and I bear it no more
Praise the Lord, praise the Lord, O my soul!

Refrain: It is well (it is well)
With my soul (with my soul)
It is well, it is well with my soul

For me, be it Christ, be it Christ hence to live:
If Jordan above me shall roll,
No pang shall be mine, for in death as in life
Thou wilt whisper Thy peace to my soul.

Refrain: It is well (it is well)
With my soul (with my soul)
It is well, it is well with my soul.

But, Lord, 'tis for Thee, for Thy coming we wait,
The sky, not the grave, is our goal;
Oh, trump of the angel! Oh, voice of the Lord!
Blessed hope, blessed rest of my soul!

Refrain: It is well (it is well)
With my soul (with my soul)
It is well, it is well with my soul.

And Lord, haste the day when my faith shall be sight
The clouds be rolled back as a scroll
The trump shall resound, and the Lord shall descend
Even so, it is well with my soul!

Refrain: It is well (it is well)
With my soul (with my soul)
It is well, it is well with my soul [19]

"Famous hymn composer, Philip Bliss (1838-1876), was so moved by Horatio's prose that he composed a peaceful tune to accompany the words. Bliss and Sankey published the song in 1876.

"It's incredible to think such encouraging and uplifting words were born from the depths of such unimaginable sorrow. It's an example of truly inspiring faith and trust in the Lord. And it goes to show the power our God has to cause us to overcome even the darkest times of our earthly lives."[20]

Appendix Three — Comfort In Worship

(To be used with Chapter Two)

How I Was Comforted at Laura's Funeral — Hebrews 12:1-2; Isaiah 49:13-16; Deuteronomy 31:8

Did you know that the Lord inhabits our praises? That means He lives in our worship of Him.

Why do we worship Him?

Because He is worthy of all our praise and all honor belongs to Him. He is our Creator.

Why is He worthy?

Jesus died for our sins on the cross.

Aren't we good people?

We have sinned. He was sinless. He took our place and suffered punishment for our sins on the cross. He ransomed us and paid for all our sins. We will not be punished for our sins if we repent.

Does the Son of God really know how we feel? How we suffer?

Yes, He was human. Jesus knows how we feel. He identifies with us. He went to Lazarus' tomb. Lazarus was Jesus' friend. Jesus wept. We can see His compassion as we read how He lived on this earth and how He spoke to people. Jesus knows how you feel.

The Soul

The soul realm is our mind, will, and emotions — grief lodges in the soul.

How is your mind today?

Jesus renews our minds.

How are your emotions today?

Jesus restores our frazzled emotions. He removes wounds in our souls.

How is your will today?

We have to line up our will with God's will then peace comes to us. Jesus is the Prince of Peace. Jesus doesn't force you to love Him. He gave you a will and wants you to choose Him as Lord of your life. He is able to comfort us as we live our lives on this earth. When we say: "I want to obey God. I want to worship the God I can see in creation. This is a beautiful world. I am going to trust God." These are examples of our will.

Through Jesus, our souls can be well!

As a father has compassion on his children, so the Lord has compassion on those who fear him.
Psalm 103:13 (NASB)

If you are new to this journey of being a Christian, or if you have been walking this path for many years, I want you to know that you are not alone in this world. Jesus promised that He would never leave you or forsake you even to the end of the age. He loves you!

A few years ago, I had a vivid dream that I still remember to this day. The dream reminded me of the line in this hymn: "when sorrows like sea billows roll." I saw myself standing in water (there were cement walls around, so it was similar to a wave pool) when suddenly a huge wave came behind me, crashed over me, and knocked me down into the water face first. After the wave passed, I saw myself stand up. I saw a second wave roll over me, and I went under the water again. I rose up again to a standing position a second time. A larger wave came the third time, swept over me, and the dream ended. It seemed that the walls were security for me, but even within the walls, the waves came and knocked me down.

As Christians, we battle unbelief, fear, trials, despair, and temptations that seem like large waves taking us by surprise and knocking us down. We receive confidence and security from Jesus. We are given many instructions in the Word of God to stand strong and rise up no matter what comes against us. Ephesians 6:13

There are several Scripture verses that will bring comfort to you if you find yourself in the midst of grief, sorrow, or depression right now. The Word of God gives us life and hope. The Bible is more than a book. It's a Holy Book, and the Words have power to change our lives.

3 John 1:2; John 14:18; Hebrews 4:12; Hebrews 13:5; Matthew 9:36; 2 Corinthians 1:4; Psalm 116:5

Appendix Four—Believers Are Called Saints

(To be used with Chapter 3 God's Faithfulness to His Loved
Ones)

**The Bible refers to believers as "Saints," "Holy Ones,"
"Blameless," "Righteous," and "Upright"** — 1 Samuel 2:9; 2
Chronicles. 6:41; Psalm 34:9; Romans 12:1; 1 Peter 2:9;
Deuteronomy. 33:1-4; Psalm 37:27-38

> *You who love the Lord, hate evil! He preserves the souls
> of His saints; He delivers them out of the hand of the
> wicked.*
> Psalm 97:10 (NKJV)

> *As for the saints who are on the earth, "They are the
> excellent ones, in whom is all my delight."*
> Psalm 16:3 (NKJV)

Appendix Five — Light

(To be used with Chapter Seven)

Jesus Is The Light Of The World — Genesis 1:3-4 Nehemiah 9:19; Matthew 6:22; Psalm 36:9; Matthew 5:14-16; John 1:6-9; Ephesians 5:8

> *Arise, shine; for your light has come! And the glory of the Lord is risen upon you. For behold, the darkness shall cover the earth, and deep darkness the people; But the Lord will arise over you, and His glory will be seen upon you.*
> Isaiah 60:1-2 (NKJV)

> *And this is the judgment, that the Light has come into the world, and people loved the darkness rather than the Light; for their deeds were evil.*
> John 3:19 (NASB)

> *"While you have the light, believe in the light that you may become sons of light."*
> John 12:36 (NKJV)

> *I have come as Light into the world, so that no one who believes in Me will remain in darkness.*
> John 12:46 (NASB)

> *But all things become visible when they are exposed by the light, for everything that becomes visible is light.*
> Ephesians 5:13 (NASB)

Appendix Six

(To be used with Chapter Seven Healing)

Praying The Word Of God For Healing — Exodus 15:26; Psalm 34:20; Psalm 103:2-3; Psalm 91:1-16; Psalm 107:20

◆ I diligently listen to your voice, Lord my God, and I choose to do what is right in Your sight.

◆ I listen to Your commandments; I choose to keep Your statutes.

◆ God, you will not allow any of the diseases to come upon me which You put on the Egyptians: for You are the Lord who heals me.

◆ I will worship the Lord my God, and his blessing will be on my food and water.

◆ The Lord will take away sickness from the midst of me.

◆ I choose to speak with the tongue of the wise to bring healing.

◆ I choose to be a faithful ambassador so that I can bring health and healing.

◆ Pleasant words are a honeycomb to the soul and health to the bones.

◆ My light will break forth like the morning; my healing shall spring forth speedily;

◆ My righteousness shall go before you; the glory of the Lord is my rear guard.

◆ God sent His Word and healed me, and He delivered me from destruction.

◆ I am beautiful and without blemish.

Appendix Seven — Most High Verses

(To be used with Chapter Ten — God's Sovereignty)

Most High Verses — 2 Samuel 22:14; Psalm 9:2; Psalm 7:17; Psalm 18:13; Psalm 21:7; Psalm 47:2; Psalm 50:14; Psalm 57:2; Psalm 77:10; Psalm 78: 17,35,56; Psalm 91:1

The world we live has many gods, little "g." There is One God who is above all gods. He commands us not to have any other God's before Him. His name is MOST HIGH. There are people who scoff at His existence:

> They say, "How does God know? Is there knowledge [of us] with the Most High?"
> Psalm 73:11 (AMP)

There is a bible story that illustrates the power of the Most High:

> For I will pass through the land of Egypt this night, and will smite all the firstborn in the land of Egypt, both man and beast; and against all the gods of Egypt I will execute judgment: I am the Lord.
> Exodus 12:12 (KJV)

> Thou shalt have no other gods before me.
> Exodus 20:3 (KJV)

> It is good to give thanks to the Lord, and to sing praises to Your name, O Most High.
> Psalm 92:1 (NKJV)

> There is a river whose streams shall make glad the city of God, the holy place of the tabernacle of the Most High.
> Psalm 46:4 (NKJV)

To live under God's shadow is to have a safe place of refuge. He has promised that we can live under His shadow. When the highest God makes a promise, we can be sure of it for our lives.

Appendix Eight — False Doctrines — Lies

(To be used with Chapter Twelve)

What we believe is so important! Satan comes to steal, kill, and destroy, but Jesus tells us that He came to give us abundant life and He came to destroy the works of the devil. None of us even want to think about the devil telling us lies. We do not realize that we believe Satan's lies, but he can present us with thoughts in our minds.

When you determine that you have believed a lie, you get a sick feeling in your gut. "I fell for it." You become discouraged with yourself. I would dare to say that lies can become a source of depression in our lives. But when you realize the truth, the truth will set you free. Believing a lie happens to all believers, but you don't have to live deceived anymore. You get to choose what you think about.

The enemy has us coming and going. If we believe the lies, he's got us (or he thinks he's got us). If we see the truth, his strategy to destroy us with depression is canceled, demolished, and made null and void. We can resist him, and we are able to cast down any confusion in our minds because Jesus came to destroy the works of the devil. We have the victory through Jesus!

You belong to Jesus, and He has not given you a spirit of fear but of power, love, and a sound mind! The Bible is our standard against lies and false doctrines. You may as well know this too, Timothy, that in the last days it is going to be very difficult to be a Christian. For people will love only themselves and their money; they will be proud and boastful, sneering at God, disobedient to their parents, ungrateful to them, and thoroughly bad. They will be hardheaded and never give in to others; they will be constant liars and troublemakers and will think nothing of immorality. They will be rough and cruel, and sneer at those who try to be good. They will betray their friends; they will be hotheaded, puffed up with pride, and

prefer good times to worshiping God. They will go to church, yes, but they won't really believe anything they hear. Don't be taken in by people like that.
2 Timothy 3:1-5 (TLB)

But the Holy Spirit tells us clearly that in the last times some in the church will turn away from Christ and become eager followers of teachers with devil-inspired ideas. These teachers will tell lies with straight faces and do it so often that their consciences won't even bother them.
1 Timothy 4:1-2 (TLB)

Endnotes

Chapter Four

[1] Notes on p.1667, note 1; Luke 1:1-2, Life Application Study Bible. Tyndale House Publishers, Inc. Wheaton, Illinois 60189 Notes and Bible Helps copyright 2004.

[2] Vital Statistics, Notes p. 1666, note 1, Special Features of Luke's Gospel. Application Study Bible, Tyndale House Publishers, Inc., Inc. Wheaton, Illinois 60189 Notes and Bible Helps copyright 2004.

[3] P. 1668 note 1, Luke 1:1-4, Life Application Study Bible, Tyndale House Publishers, Inc. Wheaton, Illinois 60189 Notes and Bible Helps copyright 2004.

[4] P. 1668, note 3, Life Application Study Bible, Tyndale House Publishers, Inc. Wheaton, Illinois 60189 Notes and Bible Helps copyright 2004

[5] P. 1668 notes, Luke 1:1-4, Life Application Study Bible, Tyndale House Publishers, Inc. Carol Stream, Illinois 60188 Notes and Bible Helps copyright 2004

[6] Tyndale House Publishers gratefully acknowledges the role of Youth for Christ/USA in preparing the Life Application Notes and Bible helps. Life Application Study Bible, Tyndale House Publishers, Inc. Wheaton, Illinois 60189 Notes and Bible Helps copyright 2004.

[7] koinoniahouse. "Characteristics of Angels - Chuck Missler." YouTube. YouTube, March 5, 2012. https://www.youtube.com/watch?v=2cB7a2_z9Z0.

Chapter Six

[8] Fire Bible, Global Study Edition, NIV,2009, Notes on Matt. 1:23 Virgin…Give birth to a son p.1672; Life Publishers International 1625 N Robberson Ave. Springfield, MO 65803 U.S.A.

[9] Fire Bible, Global Study Edition, NIV,2009, Notes on Virgin…Give Birth to a Son (2) p.1673; Life Publishers International 1625 N Robberson Ave. Springfield, MO 65803 U.S.A.

[10] Godsaidmansaid.com. "Prophecies of Christ and Proof That God Is." // Prophecies of Christ and Proof that God Is - GODSAIDMANSAID.COM. Accessed June 28, 2021. https://www.godsaidmansaid.com/topic3.asp?Cat2=256&ItemID=1174.

Chapter Seven

[11] Adapted from material copyright 2020 Used by permission Steve and Beth Poll.

Chapter Nine

[12] From Guideposts Magazine, Copyright 1972 by Guideposts Associates, Inc, Carmel, New York 10512. Good News Publishers/A nonprofit corporation, 1300 Crescent Street/Wheaton, Illinois. Used with permission all rights reserved on 12/10/20.

Poem

[13] Copyright Russell Kelfer. All rights reserved. Used by permission Martha Kelfer (widow). Dec. 2020

Chapter Ten

[14] Sovereignty of God p. 969 The New Nave's Topical Bible; 1969, Regency Reference Library, Zondervan Publishing House, 1415 Lake Drive, S.E. Grand Rapids, MI 49506

[15] The New Nave's Topical Bible, *Sovereignty of God* p. 969 Nave, Orville J., and Edward Viening. *The New Nave's Topical Bible*. Grand Rapids, MI: Zondervan Pub. House, 1983.

[16] "G1413 - Dynastēs - Strong's Greek Lexicon (nasb20)." Blue Letter Bible. https://www.blueletterbible.org/lang/lexicon/lexicon.cfm?Strongs=G1413&t=NASB20.

Appendix Two

[17] History.com Editors. "Chicago Fire of 1871." History.com. A&E Television Networks, March 4, 2010. (Updated: August 21, 2018). https://www.history.com/topics/19th-century/great-chicago-fire.

[18] Nola Mae VanWagenen, Gena Philibert-Ortega, LeAnne, Sir BC Nwosu, and Ray Williams. "'It Is Well with My Soul': the Story of Horatio Spafford." GenealogyBank Blog. https://blog.genealogybank.com/it-is-well-with-my-soul-the-story-of-horatio-spafford.html.

[19] Attribution: It Is Well With My Soul - Lyrics, Hymn Meaning and Story. Copyright status is Public Domain; Phillip P. Bliss, 1876 *Horatio G. Spafford, 1873*
"It Is Well With My Soul - Lyrics, Hymn Meaning and Story." GodTube. Accessed June 28, 2021. https://www.godtube.com/popular-hymns/it-is-well-with-my-soul/

[20] "It Is Well With My Soul - Lyrics, Hymn Meaning and Story." GodTube. Accessed June 25, 2021. https://www.godtube.com/popular-hymns/it-is-well-with-my-soul/

For further research:

Cook, Steven R. "A Biblical Worldview." Thinking on Scripture, June 6, 2021. https://thinkingonscripture.com/a-biblical-worldview/

Dr. Tony Evans. "Tony Evans Speaks on Strength in Your Struggles (Preached 02/02/2020)." YouTube. YouTube, February 5, 2020. https://www.youtube.com/watch?v=D8A26qdp3Yk.

Janssen, Ian, Steven B. Heymsfield, ZiMian Wang, and Robert Ross. "Skeletal Muscle Mass and Distribution in 468 Men and Women Aged 18–88 Yr." Journal of Applied Physiology, July 1, 2000. https://journals.physiology.org/doi/full/10.1152/jappl.2000.89.1.81.

"Keyword Search: Sovereign." BibleGateway. https://www.biblegateway.com/quicksearch/?quicksearch=sovereign&qs_version=NIV.

Rogers, Sy. The Man In The Mirror. https://www.exodusglobalalliance.org/themaninthemirrorp338.php.

Vine, W. E., Merrill F. Unger, and William White. *Vine's Complete Expository Dictionary of Old and New Testament Words: with Topical Index*. Chattanooga, TN: AMG Publishers, 1998.

Made in the USA
Middletown, DE
17 December 2021

54053082R00144